WOOD CARVING
MADE EASY

WOOD CARVING MADE EASY

BY ALAN HOFFSOMMER

TAB BOOKS

BLUE RIDGE SUMMIT, PA. 17214

FIRST EDITION

FIRST PRINTING—JANUARY 1980

Copyright © 1980 by TAB BOOKS

Printed in the United States of America

Library of Congress Cataloging in Publication Data
Hoffsommer, Alan.
   Wood carving made easy.

   Includes index.
   1. Wood-carving.   I. Title.
TT199.7.H63   736'.4   79.22981
ISBN 0-8306-9732-2
ISBN 0-8306-1170-3 pbk.

Contents

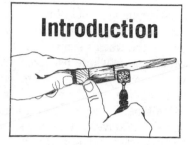

Introduction

As a boy, a most vivid recollection stands out in my mind. Whenever I visited my grandfather out on his Kansas farm, he would never fail to get out his pocket knife and make me a whistle. To this day, I can't remember what he made it from, but it was always the same shape and size. We would walk down behind the barn where there was a windbreak of hedge trees growing along the lane out to the pasture. From among the underbrush, he would select what always looked like a tall weed and would cut it off. We would go back to the house to sit on the back porch where he would proceed to make the whistle. The inside was a very soft material which was easily hollowed out. Then a notch was cut in the top and the underside cut at a slant to make the mouthpiece.

FIRST EXPERIENCES WITH WOOD CARVING

After testing it out to make sure it worked, he gave it to me and the knife went back in his pocket. With the whistle in my mouth, I was off, running wildly down the lane and out into the pasture where I shattered the silence of the desolate Kansas countryside. I wasn't satisfied until I had pierced the eardrums of every cow, horse and jack rabbit in sight.

As I became older, I was allowed to visit my grandfather for several weeks at a time by myself. He was a widower and at the time, when on those visits, it seemed we were the only two people in the world. We were two marooned souls, adrift alone on a sea of wheat fields, surrounded by a shore line of hedge trees. He wasn't given much to talking and we spent many hours sitting on that back porch, listening to a silerce so loud it almost hurt you ears.

But Saturday afternoons always included a visit to town where we secured our weekly supply of provisions. It was a very small town with only several stores, a church, a school and the ever present garage and service station. As small as it was, it was always a treat after being by ourselves all during the week. The most amazing thing about that town was the manner in which other people appeared from out of nowhere, almost as if by magic. After buying the week's supplies, I would sit atop a barrel in front of the general store where I savored my weekly stick of candy. The men would slowly gather around to sit on boxes or on the steps and the conversation would start. Of course, the whittling started at the same time. Everyone had a knife. There were big knives, little knives, fat knives and skinny krives. Most of the knives had black, shiny handles, some with a bright, metal shield embedded in the side. Once in a while, you would see a knife with a pearl handle. One man had a knife with a pale, red handle which sparkled in the sunlight.

The farmers always seemed able to produce a stick of wood, amazingly all about the same size. I never knew what they talked about as they whittled, but I'm sure it had something to do with the rain they didn't get, the rain which was sure to come and how the crops were coming along. I was too fascinated by the array of beautiful knives to be interested in something so trivial as conversation. Sometimes they would have a contest to see who could whittle up a stick with the most shavings without any coming loose from the stick. Other times they just whittled away and let the shavings fall where they may. It was fun to watch the piles of shavings which grew between the feet of the men as the afternoon wore on. Then, one by one, the men would squint up at the sun, fold up their knives and wander off down the street to their cars where the womenfolk were waiting. We were always the last to leave as we didn't have any womenfolk to shuffle their feet impatiently in the dirt, wanting to get home and start supper. We could go home and eat anytime we wanted.

At about this age, I was allowed to handle that knife by myself. The back porch from where we sat and watched the sun go down was made, as were the steps, from huge slabs of sandstone. Off to one side of the porch was an indentation, worn perfectly smooth from years of knife sharpening. My grandfather never said anything, but he always made sure I was watching as he sharpened his knife. One evening he gave me the knife and told me to sharpen it for him. The excitement of the moment was almost too much to bear. But I set about my task and began to copy the slicing, sliding movements across the stone with the blade of the knife as I had watched my grandfather do so many times before. When I thought I had gone through the motions properly, I handed the knife back to him with trembling hards and watched as he tested the blade against his thumb. It must have been satisfactory as he gave a nod of approval and the ever present stick came out of his pocket. One by one, the shavings started falling to the ground, each one almost exactly the same shape and size as the others.

At undetermined intervals, he would stop and inspect his stick as if it were a great work of art. He might as well have been a Michelangelo pausing to inspect the progress of his greatest work of sculpture. As always, the last shaving would fall to the ground as the sun disappeared behind the hills, and I would know it was time to go in and fix our supper.

Those were magical moments spent there on the back steps. As the evening wore on, the silence grew into a chorus of sounds not too many people get to hear in this day and age. There was the clucking and fussing of the chickens as they settled down on their roosts for the night. A little more distant was the grunting of the pigs, interrupted by an occasional squeal as one of the little ones was crowded out from his place for dinner. We also heard the stomping of the horses' hoofs as they gathered, each one at his own stall, for his daily ration of oats.

Almost as if there was a given signal, the locusts and crickets started to sing, adding their voices to the symphony. The wind, which had been present and taken for granted all day long, now started to moan around the eaves of the house. As it started to grow a little darker from the setting of the sun, small cottontail rabbits could be seen hopping hesitantly up through the grass to sit at a distance. Watching our movements, nibbling a blade of grass, it seemed as if the rabbits were sharing some mysterious, spiritual companionship with us. They seemed unafraid and never bothered to move when we got up to go into the house.

From the hills in the distance could be heard the yelping and barking of the coyotes. From a greater distance yet, you might catch the mournful howl of an occasional wolf. To many people, that setting might have been frightening and lonely, even depressing, but never to me. I would experience an immense feeling of happiness and well-being. I suppose this was partly because I could sense that

...e feeling in my grandfather. I don't ever remember him carving ...t anything in his life, except that whistle, but he must have derived a great feeling of calm and satisfaction from whittling on a stick. Turning it over and over in his hand, feeling the warm, smooth texture of the wood, sometimes he would stop and inspect the stick after every slice of the blade. He knew that each time he made a cut, the stick was changing in shape and size.

And that's what this book is all about!

WOOD CARVING AS AN ART FORM

As a form of art, wood carving ranks right up there with the best. I think it would be safe in assuming that wood carving predates most forms of sculpture. Long before man had made tools efficient enough to work on stone, his stone knives and axes were sharp enough to cut wood. However, because wood will deteriorate and rot when not properly taken care of, we will never know at what stage man started carving objects out of wood. If time, wind and erosion can wear down some of the great stone wonders in Egypt, you might well imagine what has happened to anything made of wood.

Have you ever noticed the difference in feeling when you walk into a room that is furnished in steel and chrome furniture than when you walk into a room with wood furniture? You will instantly get a feeling of warmth and friendliness from a room with wood furnishings, while the other will leave you with a sterile, cold impression that is hard to ignore. This same feeling of warmth comes to anyone who likes to work with wood.

I don't mean to imply that a stone sculpture or an oil painting is a cold, calculating form of art. Each artist has his own medium through which he wishes to express himself or convey an idea. It is the product of the artist's imagination itself which leaves the viewer with one impression or another. However, there seems to be a special bond between the wood carver and the material with which he works. It may be because he knows the wood was once a living, breathing creature which grew from a tiny seed into a large, sturdy tree. And like humans themselves, each tree is an individual, not one growing exactly like another. Each piece of wood has its own grain pattern (personality) which the artist attempts to incorporate into his work.

In our mechanized society, wood carving as a profession is largely a thing of the past. Huge, computerized lathes are used to turn out the endless variety of wood products we use. The wooden art forms found in gift shops which are produced in this country are almost entirely produced on a lathe. Even the simple axhandle is machine-made. You place a piece of wood in a lathe and fasten it into place. Press a button and sharp, steel cutters begin to grind away. Relays click, cams fall into place, the bits move along a preset pattern and presto! You have a gun stock, a salad bowl or a wooden banana.

This technology leaves room for only a few wood finishers or hand craftsmen of a special need. Artists or hobbyists are the only ones left to take a piece of wood and work it into shape by hand, guided only by the spark of an idea in their minds and the feel of their fingers.

Most people think that it takes a gifted artist to make a wood carving worthy of notice. Nothing could be further from the truth. True, there are a few people who seem to be born with an artistic sense and there are a few who cannot seem to master any form of art. But both types are the exception rather than the rule. The same applies to any exceptional person, whether in the field of mathematics, astrology or art. There aren't too many Michelangelos or Einsteins to be found. Rather, it is a matter of study and practice, practice, practice, and then more study. It is the desire to accomplish something, rather than an inborn ability, which makes an artist, musician or mathematician.

STEPS IN WOOD CARVING

Many people lack only an idea of where to start. They would like to try carving something out of wood, but don't know what to carve. I had one woman tell me she would like to try wood carving, but didn't have any idea of what she should start with. The first step in wood carving is to have something in milnd. It doesn't make any difference whether you want to copy something or whether you want to make an original. The idea must be there to begin with.

The next step is to know what your subject looks like. You decide you want to carve out a chipmunk, but when it comes down it it, you really don't know what a chipmunk looks like. The whole project falls apart before it gets started. One of the subjects an art student studies is anatomy. To properly draw, paint or make a sculpture of the human body, one must know what it looks like, how the muscles are shaped and the size of one region of the body as compared to another. The same things apply if you want to carve a chipmunk. You must know what it looks like or it may turn out to look like a skunk. Do you have a favorite bird or flower you want to carve?

To test yourself, sit down and make a drawing of it without looking at a picture. This will tell you if you really know what it looks like or if you just have a vague impression, Knowing how to handle a knife, chisel or sanding drum is not, in itself, enough to produce a wood carving. The tools you use in making your carving are simple extensions of your mind.

PSYCHOLOGY BEHIND WOOD CARVING

Teaching someone to make wood carvings from a book is an impossible task. You can't sit down and read a book on mathematics and instantly become a mathematician. The same thing applies to a book on wood carving. You must be the teacher yourself, using the book as a guide. You must study the material, take a piece of wood in hand, work with it and get the feel of the tools you are using. I do not consider myself an expert in wood carvirg. Rather, I consider myself someone who gets enjoyment from it that I want to pass along some of my enthusiasm and a few of my ideas. We will stay away from the so-called "traditional" wood carving. To me, wood carving is making something out of wood, by hand, no matter what tools or method you use. Anything goes!

A lot of people are scared away from wood carving by the usual publicity photograph of the bearded wood carver, wearing his leather apron, chipping away at a huge log with a large mallet and chisel. This is not the way you start out in wood carving. You have to crawl before you learn to walk. I am going to go through the process of making some simple wood carvings, including photographs as I go along to give you an idea of how the carving progresses and what it looks like from one stage to the next. Obviously, I can't take a picture at every stage of the carving as the piece of wood is constantly changing in shape. I will try to talk you through some simple carvings just as a flight instructor would "talk" his student through a landing. I will attempt to tell you how I go about the carving and how I think and feel as I work. Some days I am just not in the mood and everything turns out wrong. On other days the shape of what I am working on seems to appear without my even concentrating on it.

The projects we will work on in this book are, naturally, things I like to carve. Most of my ideas have come from seeing something I liked in a store which I thought I could make myself and/or improve upon. All the designs are my own. Many of them have been changed two or three times as I saw room for improvement. As I copy something I have seen and incorporate my own changes into it, this leads me to start a design entirely of my own. If you really work your way through this book and try each carving, even pick out and work on the ones you like best, you will develop ideas of your own. You will find that one project leads you into another. And this is really what I am trying to accomplish. There are many ways to use your wood carving talent, things you can make to use around the house or decorate with as you wish. That is what wood carving should be about. Make something which will express an idea you want to get across or make something you can use. You will obtain a lot more satisfaction from making a set of coasters you can use when guests are around than you will from carving the most beautiful figure in the world, which doesn't mean anything to you.

I guess what I am getting around to is the psychology behind wood carving. I have a variety of hobbies, but the ones which interest me most are the ones I try to investigate a little deeper. Because I am interested, I am compelled to try. I follow patterns, but I am not ruled by them. The patterns I have included in this book are only guides, ideas to give you a point at which to start. I have tried to include a wide enough variety of projects that each person might find something suitable to work on. After you have copied a few, you might want to deviate from them to suit your own fancy. Making a copy is good practice, but the real pleasure in wood carving is in developing your own ideas, which leads you to making your own patterns. As you progress with your wood carving ability, you will constantly be on the watch for things you might wish to carve. Gift shops and magazines are full of things which you might get an idea from, things you might want to copy or improve upon to suit your own taste. You will see a block of wood and instantly you will know it is just the right size and shape for something you have been wanting to make.

After you get into this book, you are probably going to wonder if you are getting into wood carving, carpentry, painting or whatever. But wood carving should be more than just carving out an owl, and another owl, and another owl. True, the more times you carve the same object, the better you become at it. But after so long a time, you begin to tire of it unless you are making a particular object for sale. After all, how many owls do you want sitting around the house?

The simplest carving techniques may be used in a wide variety of projects. A good example of this is inletting. By inletting, I mean carving out a section from one piece of wood into which another piece of wood, or other object, will fit perfectly. Although a simple technique, it takes considerable skill and patience to set one piece of wood into another so that the edges fit perfectly.

The proper way to use this book is to read the entire table of contents first before starting any project. I hope you will find this is a book, not only on how to carve something, but on how to use your carving skill to decorate many different objects with the same or similar carving. You will most probably find me repeating myself throughout this book, but they are things I want to impress upon your mind. If you get a little bored wading through all the trivia you find in learning how to make a letter opener, please forgive me. It is only because I sometimes get carried away in my enthusiasm. One of the greatest pleasures in life is to share something you like with someone else. I hope you will get as much pleasure making some of the projects in this book as I have had in its preparation.

Alan Hoffsommer

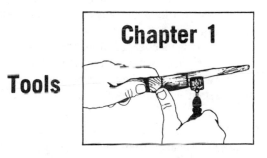

Chapter 1

Tools

You have two tools you will use more than any others, your thumb and a piece of sandpaper. Once you really get into wood carving, you will find yourself spending more time using a piece of sandpaper than anything else. And, strangely enough, it is a most important part of wood carving. You can always tell a wood carver by his worn, wrinkled fingers and a thumb which is slightly lopsided. You will find sandpaper is useful in cutting, shaping and finishing. For this reason, it is important you know the different grades of sandpaper and the proper time to use each one. This, like anything else, comes with experience. As we get into the actual carving, we will go more into the uses of sandpaper.

There are several different types of carving just as there are many different styles of the carvings themselves. As I previously stated, we are going to stay away from the traditional wood carving where the actual work is done almost entirely with the mallet and chisel. Another type of wood carving is whittling. I know of at least one college that is now offering a course in whittling. Here, the entire project is carved, or whittled, out with a knife.

MOTO-TOOL

We are going to use a little of each technique, but the main tool we will use for our carving is the Dremel *Moto-tool* or similar product. In my opinion, the Moto-tool is the best thing for carving since the invention of the knife. You can accomplish as much with it as you can with all the other carving tools put together, and much more quickly. There are, naturally, some exceptions to this statement and we will go into those later. You can purchase the Moto-tool from most hobby, variety and department stores. You will find it with several different trade names, but they are all the same thing. Although it is not necessary, I would recommend getting the variable-speed tool which comes in a kit, complete with a sanding drum and an assortment of cutters. You will find a use for almost all of them in your work. Obtain any extra cutters as you go along and find the need for them.

You can get a cheaper Moto-tool separately which has only one speed, with which you may prefer to start out. However, you will find there are times when a slow speed is desirable when you are using certain types of wood or in making a specific cut.

JIGSAW

Dremel also puts out a small power *jigsaw* which is invaluable in cutting out projects. A hand-held *coping saw* will do the job, but if you are going to do much carving, you will find you are able to do the job much more quickly and neater with the power jigsaw. For thicker material and some types of hardwood, I find a sabre saw much better to use.

Your Dremel jigsaw has a power take-off on the right side of the saw where you can attach a buffing, sanding or grinding wheel. As an accessory, you can also get a flexible shaft which fastens to the power take-off and has a chuck on the end to hold your cutters and sanders. It has a smaller hand grip than does the Moto-tool and is much more efficient. Another important feature is that it doesn't get hot after a few moments of use as does the Moto-tool. It has one bad feature in that the flexible shaft runs out of the right side of the saw and necessitates your bringing the shaft around to the front of the saw in actual use. However, it is handier to use in carving than the Moto-tool. I always keep the flexible shaft on hand, although I don't use it much.

WEN HOBBY CENTER

The most convenient carving tool I have found is the *Wen Hobby Center*. As with the others, it comes under several trade names. I purchased mine from Montgomery Ward. I use this tool more than the others because it fits into my workshop better, as the flexible shaft runs from the left side of the table-mounted motor. Also, the hand grip is better designed for both rough and intricate work. It also comes with an assortment of cutters and a sanding drum which you can add to as the need arises.

KNIVES

For knives, I use *X-acto* tools. These may be purchased separately or by the set. There are several sizes of sets available with varying assortments of knife blades, chisels and gouges. For the probably want to add to your collection each time you find a particular need. Most wood carvers like to make their own knives. This is more a matter of pride than utility as it takes a lot of work and skill to make a good carving knife. However, it does make a good project for the dedicated wood carver and there are a number of books available on this subject. If you are going to work on a large project which requires using a knife, the X-*acto* knives are a little small. Making your own knife would be preferable. Larger carving knives may also be purchased from some craft stores.

VACUUM SWEEPER

A most important piece of equipment for the type of carving we will be doing is the *vacuum sweeper*. As your electric sanding drum will be creating a lot of fine sawdust, it will be necessary to have some way of controlling it. Working over the open end of a sweeper tube is ideal for this purpose. For years, I have used an old cannister type sweeper to suction off the dust, holding the open end of the tube between my knees and working over my lap. The new shop-vacs provide a lot more suction and a larger capacity tank to hold your waste.

Instead of discussing each separate knife, cutter or sanding drum now, it is easier to show you what I am using as we get into the actual carving. You will establish your own preferences after you have been doing some carving.

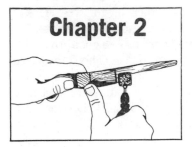

Chapter 2

The Work Area

In my opinion, your work area can be every bit as important as your tools. Clean, pleasant surroundings are conducive to good work. Although I have spent a great deal of my life in moving from one place to another, I have always managed to set aside a small spot where I could work on the hobby I was engaged with at the time. Sometimes I had room for a workshop. Other times I had nothing more than one end of a room set aside for that purpose. My workbench was, at times, nothing more than a card table set up in one end of the living room. I realize not every one is going to want to work on their wood carvings in their living room. I have always said our house was furnished in "early confusion." I believe a house is meant to be lived in, not just a showplace where you receive guests.

Because most of the carving we are going to do will produce a lot of fine sawdust, you will want to set up a work area away from the rest of the house. Naturally, a basement is the ideal place and is where I have my shop set up now. An unused bedroom is another spot you might utilize. If you live in a warm climate, one end of a screened-in porch might make a good work area, if it is sheltered from the weather.

WORKBENCH

Figure 2-1 shows the workbench which suits my purpose best. It is long enough to give me plenty of room for larger projects and it can hold several projects under way at the same time. My jigsaw is

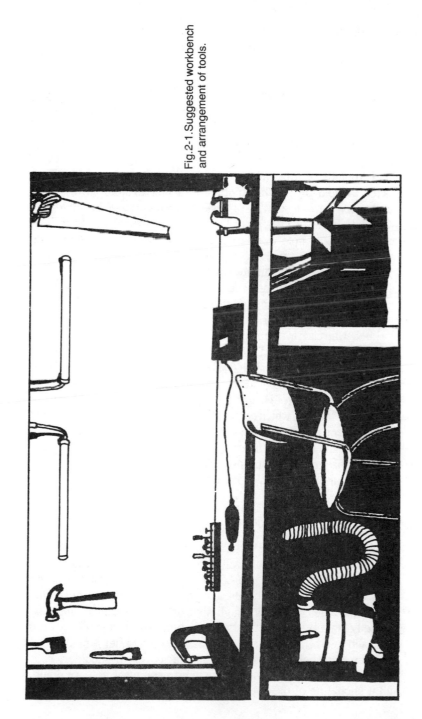

Fig. 2-1. Suggested workbench and arrangement of tools.

21

set up on the left end and a vise is on the right. Note the shop-vac under the bench. The suction tube runs up to a hole I have cut in the top of the bench. The hole is a size which allows the end of the tube to be firmly wedged into place, but not fastened permanently. This makes an ideal area on which to work. If you keep your hands over the suction area as you work, very little sawdust will escape being drawn into the shop-vac. The hobby center is placed to the right of the suction hole so that the flexible shaft may be used without having to bend it in too sharp a curve.

I kept three other objects under the bench. One is a waste basket to hold my trash. Another is a box to hold all my used sandpaper. You will soon learn never to throw a piece of sandpaper away until it gets to the point where it is absolutely smooth. The other is a box to hold wood scraps. In cutting out a figure on your jigsaw, you will always have a large variety of shapes and sizes of scraps. These scraps can always be used in making jewelry or in inletting a small figure into another piece of wood.

Keeping your workbench clean and free of clutter is not just a matter of neatness or pride. If you're not careful, you will have a workbench so cluttered up you can't find the cutter or knife blade you want, and you will spend more time looking for tools than you do using them. Your knives should always be kept in a rack. If you have purchased a set which comes in a chest, they should be replaced as soon as you are through using them. A simple way to store the cutters and sanders which come with your Moto-tool is to cut a 2 × 4 the length you think you will need. Then drill several rows of holes of a size to fit the shank of the cutters. The ones I use most often are placed in the front row, so I never have to waste time looking for a particular one when I am changing cutters or sanders.

LIGHTING

Lighting is very important. You will want to have sufficient light, but not so much as to create a glare. I sometimes place a small lamp at the back of my bench so it will create a shadow on the object I am working on. This way I can tell if I am getting a good, smooth surface. If your light is so bright that you have no shadows at all, you might miss seeing a small rough spot on an area which should be perfectly smooth. Another light I sometimes use is a medium-sized light bulb in a reflector stand such as a photographer would use. I place the stand behind me so the light shines over my shoulder. Your overhead light should be bright enough to see what you are doing, and it should be of the soft light type.

COMFORT CONSIDERATIONS

However you decide to fix up your work area, make sure it fits your particular needs and that you are comfortable. Nothing is worse than having to sit in an uncomfortable position or hold your hands at an awkward angle when you are working. The suction hole in your workbench should be cut about 8 inches back from the front of the bench. This gives you plenty of room to rest your hands as you work, but it is not so far back that you have to stretch your arms out to keep your hands over the hole. You will soon learn to keep your hands in the proper position as you work. You have only to forget it for a moment before you realize you have sawdust flying up in your face. During the summer months, I work on a lot of projects out in the back yard. Of course, this requires you to use the Dremel Moto-tool unless you want to set up a card table or something on which to set your Wen Hobby Center. If you have a picnic table in your back yard, this will provide a suitable workbench. You can work on your wood carving and get a sun tan at the same time, and the summer breezes will carry away the sawdust.

SAFETY MEASURES

As with all power tools, the instructions will tell you to wear safety glasses. I wear corrective lenses for close work and find they are satisfactory. In fact, the only time I have ever noticed any trouble along this line is when I put on a new sanding drum. There are always some loose pieces of grit which will fly off when you first start using it. If you don't wear corrective lenses, it would be advisable to use safety glasses as it is better to be safe than sorry.

If you are working in a confined area and are having trouble suctioning off the sawdust, it would be wise to wear a gauze face mask which may be purchased from most lumber, hardware or medical supply houses. I have never found it necessary to use one as it is more convenient to set up a good suction system.

Work over your suction hole at all times, even when sanding by hand or using a knife or chisel. The chips or dust which don't get sucked down the tube can easily be brushed over the hole with a shop brush or a medium-size paint brush. When sanding, stop every so often and brush the excess sawdust from your project with a small paint brush. If you brush the sawdust into your suction hole, you are accomplishing two things at once. You get a better view of what you are doing and you are keeping your work area clean. Don't blow the dust from your carving as you will have to clean it up later. Keeping good work habits will prevent you from having to stop every so often just to clean up your bench. When you are through working for the day, your work area will be almost as clean as when you started.

Just how elaborate a work area you want to set up is up to you. But if you're like most hobbyists, your work area and tools are almost as important as the project you are making.

Working From Scale Drawings

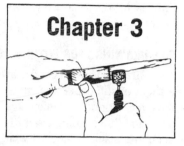

Chapter 3

Most craftsmen are acquainted with the scale drawing. It is simply a way to reduce the size of a pattern so it will fit into the pages of a book, which is smaller than the size of the actual pattern. For those of you who have never used the scale drawing, I want to include just a few simple words of instruction on the subject.

MAKING THE DRAWING

The *scale drawing* is a pattern of an object drawn over a series of vertical and horizontal lines an equal space apart, creating a series of squares. Someplace on your drawing it will tell you how far apart to draw your lines. After you have laid out your series of lines to create the pattern of squares, it is simply a matter of drawing in the object you are copying so that the lines of the object cross through the squares at the same angle and place as they do in your scale drawing. A little practice at this and you will soon be able to copy any object laid out on a scale drawing. The series of squares is most commonly referred to as a grid.

Figure 6-2, the first scale drawing in this book, is drawn over a grid of 1-inch squares, as are all the other scale drawings included. To make a full-sized pattern for this project, measure your lines off with a ruler on a blank sheet of paper and draw them in. Then start drawing in your project pattern by copying the curves and lines from the smaller grid in the book. You don't have to be an artist by any means to make an accurate copy.

This method of making a pattern can be used in another manner. Suppose you see something in a magazine you think would make a good carving project, but it is shown in a size different from what you would like. Simply draw a grid over the picture, using any size squares you wish. Then lay out a grid on a blank sheet of paper, using smaller squares if you want to reduce the size of the object, or larger squares if you want to increase the size. For those of you who don't think you can draw, you will be surprised how quickly this method can teach you to actually draw something without using the grid method.

FILE DRAWINGS FOR FUTURE USE

After you have a good drawing, it would be wise to copy it off on a sheet of stiff paper and cut it out to be filed away for future use. I have a desk drawer which contains all the different patterns I have used and those I might want to use in the future. I cut mine out of economy blank cardboard which can be obtained from most art or book stores. This material is thick enough so the edges won't get frayed or worn from drawing around it a number of times.

Having a good pattern is the first step in making a good carving for most of the projects I am including here. If you have any trouble making your pattern, just practice for a while and you will get it. Don't be satisfied with a sloppy pattern. While your actual carving will correct any mistakes you have made in the pattern, you will spend less time on it if your pattern is correct in every line.

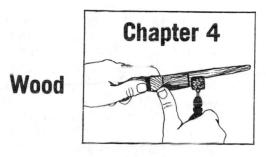

Chapter 4

Wood

When you come right down to it, wood is a most amazing substance. If you don't count the plants which we use to eat and sustain human life itself, wood is the most useful and valuable resource to man. Forests protect our land from erosion and give shelter to our wildlife. Without forests, we would not have enough oxygen to breathe. Trees are harvested and cut into the lumber with which we build our homes. Inside those homes we burn wood in a fireplace to keep warm. Our furniture and the table we eat from are made of wood. The waste materials from wood are turned into an endless variety of products, including the paper to make this book you are reading. The fruits and nuts we eat come from trees. We use trees to landscape our homes and yards to make them more beautiful.

At the rate we use wood and its by-products, it is quickly becoming one of our most precious and expensive commodities. You have only to go to the lumberyard and check the prices to prove this point. Some types of lumber are becoming so scarce that you have trouble finding them even if you are able to afford the price.

During the early days of our country, and even not so long ago, lumbering was practiced so indiscriminately that we now find ourselves trying all sorts of conservation measures to build our forests back up again. You may think this has nothing to do with wood carving, but you're wrong. Just wait until you try to find a particular kind of wood you want and see what you have to pay for a few feet of clear lumber. As an example, a large number of lumber yards don't even handle redwood any more, even if they could get it, because it is too expensive. Competition for acquiring wood is becoming a fast moving business. Some wood product businesses send representatives out to bid on anything from a single tree to a whole forest before it is even ready to harvest.

HARDWOODS AND SOFTWOODS

All wood is divided into two classes: softwoods and hardwoods. This classification is very misleading to the layman as some hardwoods are softer than softwoods and some softwoods are harder than hardwoods. An easy way to separate the two classes is to remember that softwoods are the conifers or needle-bearing trees and hardwoods are broad-leafed trees such as oak or maple. For your general information, Table 4-1 is a list of the principal hardwoods and softwoods grown in the United States.

Everyone who gets into wood carving will sooner or later want to carve something out of walnut because of its beautiful color. Although a little hard to work with for the beginner, it is ideal to carve because it does not split easily and can be worked into fine and intricate lines. Plain old white pine is the most popular wood to start out with because it is soft and easy to work.

There really isn't any need to go into the properties of all the different woods because you will learn them yourself from experience. I have my own favorites I like to work with, depending on what I am making. The availability of certain woods has a lot to do with my selections. But the beautiful part of carving with the Moto-tool is that you can carve any wood without having to worry about it being easy to split or being too hard. You can pick the wood you want because of its color, grain pattern or whatever, but they will all carve about the same with the Moto-tool. The only difference you will find is that it will take you a little longer to work down a piece of wood which is hard in texture.

SELECTING WOOD

Almost all the projects in this book can be made from standard cuts of lumber which can be purchased from your local lumber yard. There are several things to remember when you make your selection of wood. When you purchase a piece of lumber from the lumber yard and ask for a 1 × 8, it is not going to actually measure 1 inch by 8 inches. Most of the time it will actually measure 3/4 inches by 7-1/2 inches. This must be taken into consideration when planning a project. Again, most of the projects shown here use the standard cut

Table 4-1. Principal hardwoods and softwoods found in the United States.

Softwoods	Hardwoods
Douglas fir	Oak
Southern pine	Red and sap gum
Ponderosa pine	Maple
White fir	Yellow poplar
Hemlock	Black gum
White pine	Beech
Cedar	Birch
Redwood	Cottonwood
Spruce	Elm
Sugar pine	Hickory
Cypress	Basswood
Larch	Ash

of lumber and you don't have to worry. However, if you were planning a carving which called for a full 1-inch thickness, you would have to go to a 2-inch piece of wood, which might actually measure anywhere from 1-1/2 inches to 1-3/4 inches, and work it down to the desired thickness. You will also find there is a lot of difference in the thickness of lumber you buy on today's market, depending on where it was milled. Some lumber yards have a *finished lumber* section where you can find, on occasion, a piece of lumber which actually measures a full 1 or 2 inches.

As you progress with your wood carving, you will most probably want to work on larger objects. Your wood must be special ordered as you are seldom able to find anything larger than a 2-inch thickness in the lumber yard. I would advise against trying to use any large pieces of wood which have just been cut from a tree unless you know how to dry them or know where you can get them dried. If you make a carving from fresh wood, it will most probably crack on you as it dries out. It is important to properly dry the wood before the carving is made.

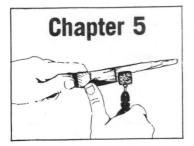

Chapter 5

Carving Techniques

Just to clarify things, I have been using the word Moto-tool, although most of the carving I do is with the Wen Hobby Center. You can call it a hand grinder, but it doesn't sound right and the words "Wen Hobby Center" are too long to use all the time. I hope I don't sound like a walking advertisement for the Dremel Company because that is not my intent or purpose. But, as I said before, the Moto-tool is the greatest thing to happen to wood carving since the invention of the knife.

BASIC GRIPS

There are two basic grips used in holding your Moto-tool. Figure 5-1 shows the grip you will use the majority of the time. You grasp the handle much the same as you would hold a tennis racket, using your thumb to steady your hand against your work. Most of the time you will draw the sanding drum toward you the same as you would draw a knife blade. Figure 5-2 shows the other grip, holding the handle as you would hold a pencil. You can see from the photographs that this method is not going to give you as much control as the other if you are using much pressure. This grip is very good when you are doing fine, intricate work which doesn't require you to put much pressure against the piece of wood you are working on.

Learning to maintain control of your Moto-tool is very important. If you are using a coarse sanding drum against a soft piece of wood, it really eats into it in a hurry. Learn to cut into your wood with

Fig. 5-1. Basic grip used in holding your Moto-tool. This method is most useful in "roughing" out a project. Use your thumb to steady your hand against your work.

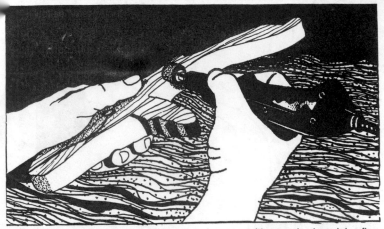

Fig. 5-2. The pencil grip allows a lighter and more positive touch when doing fine or intricate work.

smooth, even strokes, the same as you would do with a knife. Don't hold the sanding drum in one place, but keep it moving at a steady pace. Maintain a steady pressure against your work so your carving will be done in smooth lines instead of lumps and bumps. Hold your Moto-tool tightly enough so it won't get away from you, but not so tight that your hand gets tired from gripping too hard. A great explanation of the grip you should maintain can be taken from the book *Scaramouche* where the fencing master was teaching Scaramouche how to hold his sword. He said the sword should be held like a delicate bird. If you grip it too tightly, you would crush it. If you held it too lightly, it would fly from your hand. This always made an impression on me and is the best way I can think of to describe your grip on the Moto-tool.

Figure 5-3 shows the position of your hands in relation to your suction hole as you work. Due to the direction of rotation of your sanding drum or cutter, the sawdust will fly towards you as you work. Keeping your hands slightly at the back of the hole and down against the table will throw the sawdust towards the hole where it will be pulled into your shop-vac. This is an important reason for getting your suction hole positioned properly in your workbench. If you have to hold your arms at an uncomfortable reach, you will find yourself constantly pulling your hands away from the hole as you work. If you are going to set up your work area as I have suggested here, it might be wise to sit down and, holding your Moto-tool just as if you were doing some carving, find just the proper position to make your hole for the length of your arms.

Fig. 5-3. Keeping your hands at the back of your suction hole as you work will more readily allow the sawdust to be drawn into your shop-vac.

MAINTAINING PRESSURE

The amount of pressure you maintain with your Moto-tool is governed by several factors. When you are first starting to rough in your project, you will want to cut in pretty fast to get your general shape. Another factor to be considered is the softness or hardness of the piece of wood you are working with. Another important factor in wood carving, whether you are using a Moto-tool, knife, chisel or piece of sandpaper, is knowing when to stop. We will talk more about this as we get started on our first project. You should know that if you are running the Moto-tool at full speed, it is turning at the rate of 25,000 revolutions per minute. If you are pressing it fairly hard against the wood or are holding it in one place, it is going to generate enough heat to scorch the wood and the sanding drum as well. If you get a "burned spot" on your project, you then have to sand it down further to get rid of the burned spot. If you are working with a piece of hard wood, it is pretty difficult to keep from scorching it just a little as you work. This is why I say it is important to know when to stop. If you do get a burned spot in your project, you want to have enough wood left in that area to sand it away without cutting in far enough to spoil the lines of your carving. Another reason is after you have to start buying more sanding drums because you have burned some, you will be more careful. Used properly, a sanding drum will last you a long time before it has to be discarded. I have used some as long as six months before they had to be thrown away, and I do a lot of carving.

THINKING ABOUT CARVING

Just a few words about carving in general before we start on our first project. Although I will be suggesting a series of steps in carving out a project, it must never be thought of in that manner. Rather, you must think of your carving as a whole. Before you ever get started, get the idea of what you want your carving to look like fixed firmly in mind. A wood carving, the same as any other work of sculpture, should be made of one graceful line flowing into another. When you are making a cut on one part of your project, think ahead of how it is going to fit into the rest of it.

In all the projects which follow, I will try to show as clearly as I can by photographs what the finished carving will look like. Next comes the scale drawing for you to draw out into a pattern and copy off on wood. Lastly, I will go through the actual carving as I would do it. Read through each project and study the photographs to get the procedure firmly in mind before you start. As each carving or project may present a different aspect or technique, take time to go through the entire book before you start any of the projects. There might be something toward the end which you can use to good advantage on some of the first projects.

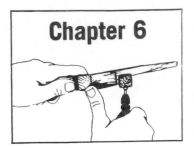

Chapter 6

Project 1—
Free-Form
Letter Opener

A favorite starting project for most wood carving books is a letter opener, and I don't want to prove an exception to the rule. It is a good way to get the feel of using your Moto-tool. You can always use a letter opener around the house and, if you make too many, they make excellent gifts for those distant relatives for whom you don't know what to buy at Christmas time. Contrary to what you may think, making a good letter opener which runs perfectly straight from one end to the other is not as easy to do as it looks. It requires you to follow that rule of thinking of your project as a whole and working on it in that manner.

Figure 6-1 shows our finished letter opener. You might call this a free-form carving. Although you have a pattern to copy and cut out, the handle of the letter opener may be carved pretty much to your own liking. I usually use a harder wood for a letter opener, but let's make this one out of white pine so you will have a soft wood on which to start working. This letter opener has been stained a Danish walnut color, and then rubbed immediately so it will have a worn, antique look. After the stain was dry, it was rubbed with Johnson's paste wax, then let dry before being buffed to a semi-gloss. This was repeated several times until the wood was thoroughly impregnated with wax.

TRACING THE PATTERN

Figure 6-2 is the scale drawing for your pattern. Lay out your 1-inch squares (grid) on a blank sheet of paper and draw in your

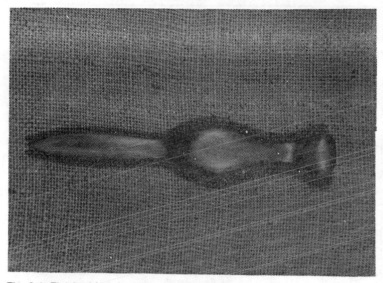

Fig. 6-1. Finished free-form letter opener.

actual size pattern. Make your pencil lines curve and cross through the squares to match the scale drawing as closely as you can. When you are satisfied you have a good drawing, cut it out and fold it over in half to see if you have drawn it as symmetrically as possible.

Trace around your pattern on a piece of clear, 1-inch white pine stock. When cutting out your project, stay to the outside of your line. This will give you a small margin for error when you are doing the carving and still allow you to keep to the original pattern in case you should carve in too far on one side or the other. After the letter opener has been cut out, draw in a pencil line, as straight as possible, completely around and in the center of the wood where it has been cut out. This will give you a reference point to work toward as you start carving (Fig. 6-3). Now draw a line across the letter opener at the point where the blade will actually stop and curve up into the handle.

If you haven't already done so, it is now time to stop and wash your hands. This isn't intended to be funny. If your hands are sweaty, oily or dirty, your project will get the oil from your hands worked into it. This is especially true when you are doing the finish sanding. If you are planning a stained finish, the stain will not blend into the wood evenly. This is probably a small point to make, but if you want your wood carvings to turn out as perfectly as possible, it is something to take into consideration. Those "small things" put

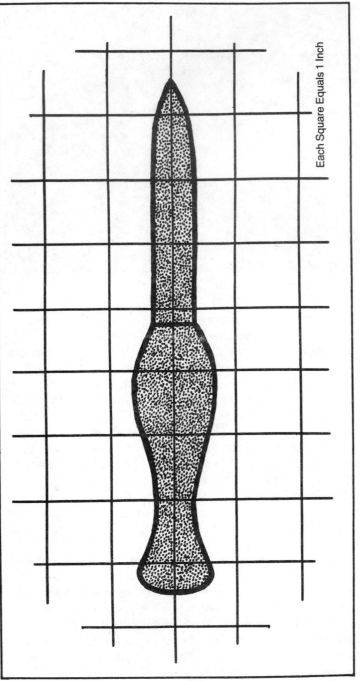

Each Square Equals 1 Inch

Fig. 6-2. Scale drawing of a free-form letter opener.

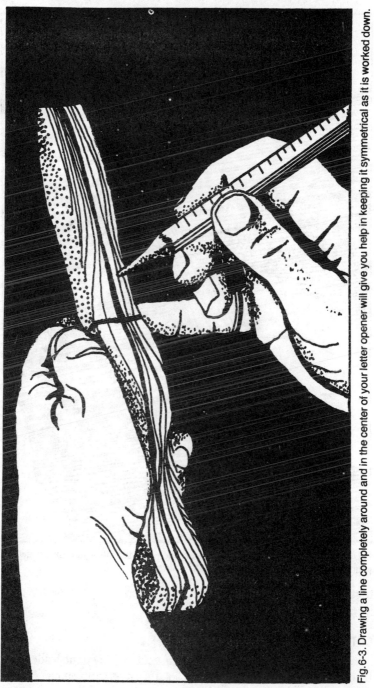

Fig. 6-3. Drawing a line completely around and in the center of your letter opener will give you help in keeping it symmetrical as it is worked down.

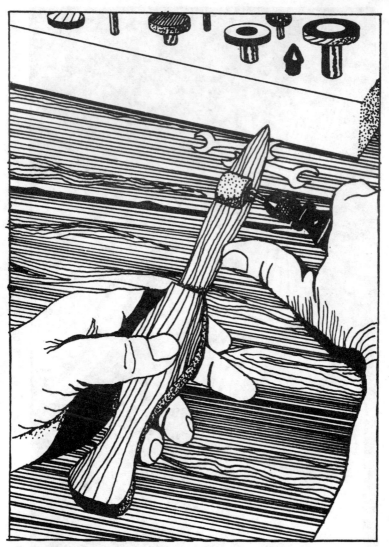

Fig. 6-4. Work the blade down evenly on each side to where you have drawn in your line to designate where the handle starts.

together make the difference between a good and a mediocre project.

CUTTING DOWN THE BLADE

Using a coarse sanding drum, start cutting down the blade first. If you have a variable speed Moto-tool, turn it on to about half speed.

As you get more used to it, you can turn it up to a higher speed. Use smooth, even strokes, first on one side, then the other. Try to cut each side down evenly as you go along instead of first cutting down one side to a given point, then the other. Don't try to cut into the wood too fast. It is more important to make each cutting stroke as smooth and even as possible. If you try to go too fast, the tendency is to leave a surface of lumps and bumps. In this case, you are required to smooth it down to obtain the desired lines on your project. So why not work it down smoothly to begin with? If you practice this right from the start, you will get into the habit of making all your cuts evenly, allowing you to work faster in the long run. You also get a better perspective of your project as a whole when you work in this manner. From start to finish, each cut should bring your carving closer to the finished product, not make it rougher. It should also be a matter of pride in your workmanship. Remember, it's all those "small things" which make the difference in your work.

Fig. 6-5 Sight down the letter opener to make sure the blade is running in a straight line from the handle. Blade should not be cut down any thinner than is shown at this time.

Figure 6-4 shows how you would cut down the blade, using your thumb to steady your hand. Cut the blade down to the point where you have drawn your line to designate where you want it to curve up into the handle. It might be wise to cut across this line with your sanding drum to make a straight cut from which to work the handle next. Stop cutting down the blade when you have it about twice as thick as it will actually be when finished. As you are cutting it down, stop frequently and sight down the handle to see if your blade is running in a straight line with the line you have drawn. If you have been working it down evenly on both sides and following your pencil line, it should appear as shown in Fig. 6-5.

Again, stop cutting when the blade is about twice as thick as you want it when finished. Don't try to narrow down the edges to a fine line at this time. That will be one of the final steps after the rest of the carving is completed.

CURVING THE HANDLE

Figure 6-6 shows the next step, that of making the handle curve down towards the blade. It should approximate the curve shown. Do this very carefully and stop before you have it down where you want it. I will probably be saying this all through the book. This is another important consideration in all the wood carvings we will do. If you cut down your project to the desired size with your rough sanding drum, you have nothing left to work with as you go from one grade of sandpaper to the other in your finish sanding. Notice we haven't been working down any of the edges up to this point. Just get the rough shape of the handle. See Fig. 6-7. Here we have started cutting in the upper part of the handle. Keep referring back to the photograph of the finished project if you must. Remember that you are working on the letter opener as a whole, not just making a series of cuts as I describe them.

We now start to work down the edges of the handle (Fig. 6-8). Keep turning it from one side to the other as you work. As you work down the edges of the handle, start working down the curve from the handle to the blade in an ever narrowing curve. As you work down this curve, very gently start narrowing down the blade, stopping to sight down the length of the letter opener to make sure your blade runs in a straight line from the center of the handle. This is very important at this stage of the carving. You will notice I have not yet rounded off the top of the letter opener. Leaving it blank up to this point will give you enough of the original piece of wood, with a pencil mark on it, to sight down.

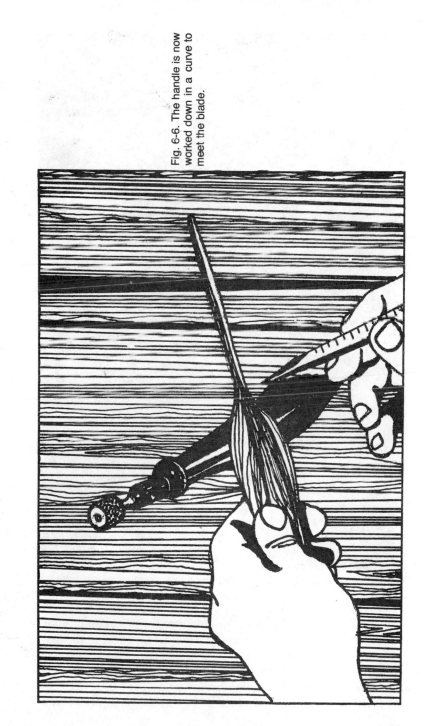

Fig. 6-6. The handle is now worked down in a curve to meet the blade.

43

Fig. 6-7. Work down the middle of the handle to a rough stage up to the top portion.

When you think you have worked down the edges sufficiently and have the curves the same on all sides, start rounding off the top. In Fig. 6-9 the pencil is pointed at the place you stopped carving before the top was rounded off as illustrated in Fig. 6-8. You now have the choice of leaving a fairly large top on it, as I have done, or cutting it down as small as you wish. However, the whole project will appear more symmetrical if you leave the same thickness in the top as you did in the wide part of the handle. Notice I have not yet worked down the blade to a fine edge.

SANDING

Now stop and change to a fine sanding drum. Start the whole process over again, using a very light touch. Keep working from one

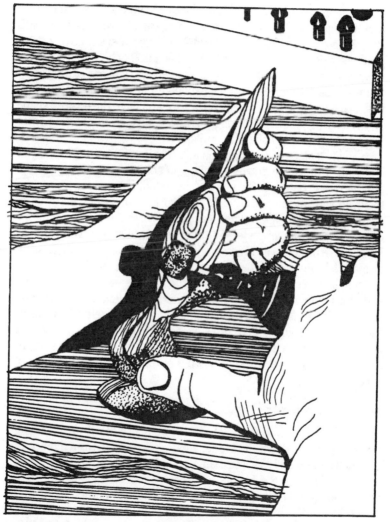

Fig. 6-8. Cut down the edges of the handle, working from one side to the other to keep it even.

side to the other. You should use your fine sanding drum only to finish up the rough carving, not in making a finished surface itself. In this step, you are only taking off the rough edges of the rough carving. Most of the time I go directly from a rough sanding drum to sanding it down by hand. In this case, it shows me I have been making my cuts smoothly and properly.

From this point on, it is simply a matter of working the project down to the desired shape and smoothness by hand, using a series of decreasingly rough grades of sandpaper. On soft woods, I start with a #80 grade of 3M *garnet* paper, then work down through each succeeding grade: 100, 120, 180 and 220. From there, I go to a #320 grade of wet or dry paper, then to 400 and 600. You want to keep in mind that sandpaper is a cutting tool. In effect, you are cutting away the wood each time you pass the sandpaper across the surface. This is the reason I keep saying to stop before you have the desired shape and size. As you keep working down the surface to get it smooth, your project gets smaller and smaller.

Using a piece of sandpaper is an art in itself. From the time you had your first lesson in woodworking in school, you were probably taught to sand only with the grain of the wood. I'm going to go against this rule and say it's not true. If you work your way down through each grade of sandpaper, when you get down to the #400 wet or dry paper, it won't have made any difference which way you sanded. Your whole project will be so smooth that the wood will actually have a shine to it. I usually cut a piece of sandpaper about 3 inches square and fold it in half to work with. Work the sandpaper against the wood with your thumb and use a pushing, twisting movement. Never sand in a straight line unless you are sanding a completely flat surface. Your thumb will conform to the surface you are working on and you won't wind up with flat spots. The only time you will sand in a straight line is when you are working down a surface, such as the blade of your letter opener.

WORKING DOWN THE BLADE

This brings us to the final step in your project. Use a sanding block in working down the blade. I have made mine from a piece of 1/2-inch lumber and it is approximately 2-1/2 5 inches in size. As you are working down the handle with each grade of sandpaper, wrap your sanding block with the same grade and work down the blade. You are using the sanding block only to keep a straight line down the length of the blade, remembering that across the width of the blade you will want it to be rounded. For this reason, you won't want to

Fig. 6-9. Work down the top portion to the desired size. The pencil is pointed at the point where you stopped working down the middle of the handle.

sand twice in the same spot. Don't try to put an edge on the blade with the rough paper, but plan your sanding so you will finally reach a sharp edge when you have worked your way down through each grade of sandpaper. Don't skip from a rough grade of sandpaper to a fine grade. Each step down from one grade to the other is necessary to take away the scratches left by previous grades. When you finally get down to the final grade of wet or dry sandpaper, you may not think you are doing much because the sandpaper is so smooth. But you are still cutting away the wood.

When you get the blade worked down to a fairly fine edge, stop and try opening an envelope to make sure it will cut the seal smoothly without tearing. There is no hard and fast rule as to how thin to make the blade. You want it thin enough to cut cleanly, but not so thin that it will be too fragile for ordinary use. If you have worked down the blade properly with each grade of sandpaper, you will have an edge which will feel sharp to your finger, even though you are using a piece of soft, white pine for your material.

Your letter opener should now be finished except for putting on the desired finish. You can stain it, paint it, leave it a natural wood color with a wax finish or put on a coat of varnish. As white pine is not a particularly pretty wood, it might be best to stain it as I did mine. If you are going to paint it, you will want to use an undercoat. After painting with your undercoat, let it dry for at least 24 hours. Then sand carefully with your finest grade sandpaper before painting.

Looking back over what you have done, you will see you could have done the same thing with a knife to get your rough shape. Then you could have finished by sanding. But by using the Moto-tool, you didn't have to worry about cutting with the grain of the wood and you probably completed your project in less ime.

Project 2 — Sea Horse Letter Opener

Chapter 7

You should now have a fair idea of how to use the Moto-tool, just how much pressure to use and what speed to set it on. You can use almost any shape or figure to make a letter opener. Our next one will be a full figure sea horse letter opener. While not too difficult, you might want to skip over this project until you have a little more experience in carving. This carving will give you good practice in trying to stay within the confines of a particular design. The design included here is not the actual shape of a sea horse, but what you might call an abstract or modern design.

Figure 7-1 is our finished project. It is cut from a piece of 1-inch birch. Birch is a harder grade of wood and it will require a little more time and patience in carving it out. Because it is a harder wood, it will get burned spots easier than the white pine if you try to go too fast, so take your time in working it down. Figure 7-2 is your scale drawing. Take your time in making the full-sized drawing, making sure the spines are properly spaced. You will notice the spine on the top of the head is in a direct line with the point of the blade, and you will want to work with this idea in mind.

After tracing around your pattern on the piece of birch, cut it out as closely as you can to the outside of your pencil line. Cutting it out as perfectly as you can will save a lot of time in your carving. Don't try to cut it too fast or your jigsaw blade will get hot and start cutting crooked. Use just enough pressure on the wood to keep it cutting as fast as the jigsaw blade will cut it. If you think it's not cutting

Fig. 7-1. Finished sea horse letter opener.

properly, stop and let the blade cool for a few moments. Then continue.

Figure 7-3 shows how we again use a pencil line down the center of the project to keep it as symmetrical as possible. You will also notice several places where the cutting was not smooth. This was a result of the blade getting too hot and starting to cut off center. After stopping to let the blade cool, you can see how it started cutting straight again.

CARVING PROCEDURES

There is no set rule as to where to start your carving, but I always start a letter opener on the blade simply because I want to take my time and make sure it runs in a straight line from the top of the head. Cut your blade down as shown in Fig. 7-4. In this carving, you will want to stop the blade in a definite, straight line where it joins the tail of the sea horse. In Fig. 7-5, we are cutting straight across the blade at this point. I use the words "straight line" to indicate it should be a right angle cut. Actually, it is slightly curved to follow the curve of the tail of the sea horse. Stop working down the blade when you have reached the approximate thickness as shown in Fig. 7-5.

Next, make a cut as shown in Fig. 7-6. This is where the tail separates from the body of the sea horse. Don't try to cut in too far at this time. As you continue to round out the body and tail later, this

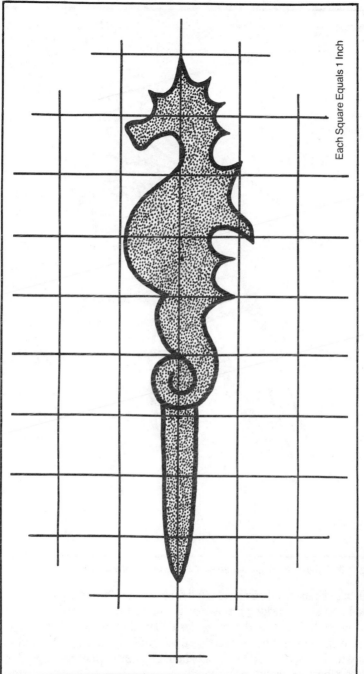

Each Square Equals 1 Inch

Fig. 7-2. Scale drawing of a sea horse letter opener.

51

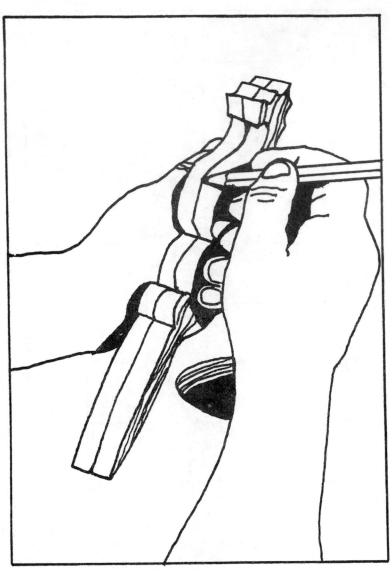

Fig. 7-3. Draw in a pencil line around the center of the project.

will take shape until you have a full rounded cut. Now move on to the head and start working it down as shown in Fig. 7-7. You will want the head to be of a thickness less than that of the body. Start narrowing down the nose so that it will finally reach a round end as shown. The spines on the head should be cut towards a point, but leave plenty of wood to work with as you finish up later.

In Fig. 7-7 the pencil is pointed towards the line which runs
the top of the fin into the curve of the body. Maintain this
throughout your carving. Refer back to Fig. 7-1. You will notice th
line gives you a point of separation between the head and the body,
and it forms the neck. At this point, don't try to round out too much in
between the spines, but just cut it down to get the general shape and
thickness of the head and neck.

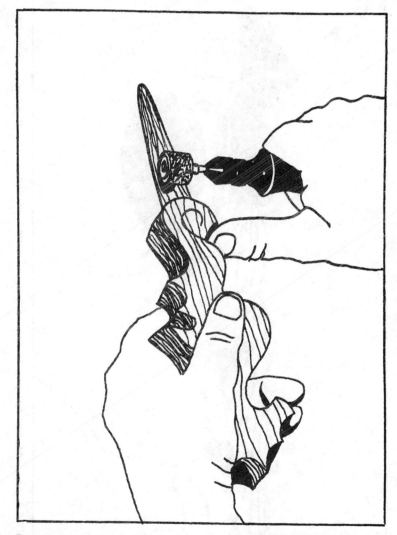

Fig. 7-4. Work each side of the blade down evenly, leaving it about twice as thick
as desired at this time.

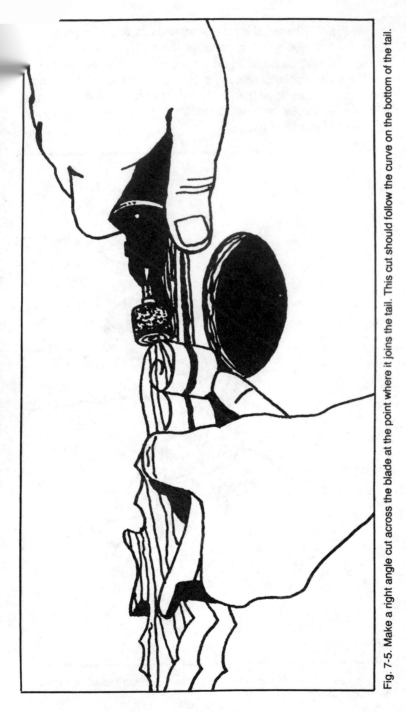

Fig. 7-5. Make a right angle cut across the blade at the point where it joins the tail. This cut should follow the curve on the bottom of the tail.

54

Move on to Fig. 7-8 for a moment. You will notice the two la[r]ge spines which make up the fin are not brought to a point. Leavin[g] them in a straight line across the width of the body gives a more representative look of the fin. Cutting these two down to a point would just be adding two more spines to the body. In Fig. 7-8 we are starting to cut in between the spines. This should be done very carefully so as not to cut down the points of the spines. The sanding drum will not fit in between the spines. If you try to cut in too far, it will cut down the points. You should also start rounding out in between the two larger points which make up the fin. This cut will be brought out further into the body than will those in between the spines, and the smallest will be those on the head. Figure 7-9 illustrates how the curve should be cut in the fin so that it is one graceful line from top to bottom. The pencil is pointed at the top of the fin where your line starts, cuts out into the body, then curves back to follow the line of the lower part of the fin.

ROUNDING OFF THE TAIL

Now move on to the back of the tail and start rounding it off as shown in Fig. 7-9. Make sure you leave a well-rounded area below the lowest spine on the body. Move on to the front part of the tail and start rounding it off. In Fig. 7-10, the front of the tail has been worked down just slightly, and we are starting to cut down the lower

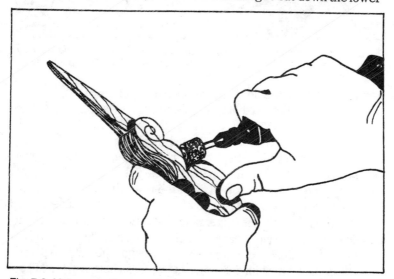

Fig. 7-6. Make a small cut in where the body separates from the tail of the sea horse. This cut should be made equally on each side.

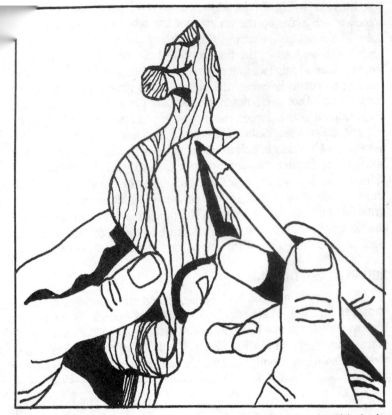

Fig. 7-7. Pencil is pointed to the line of separation between the neck and the body of the sea horse. Head and neck have been narrowed down to a rough stage.

part of the tail. Each side of the tail should be cut down as evenly as possible. Your cut should stop on the upward sweep of the tail as shown.

Figure 7-11 illustrates how the tail should be cut in at the back. Flare it out a little wider at the bottom; then wind up at the original thickness of the wood at the top front of the tail. Figure 7-12 shows how it will appear when viewed from the front. It will actually look like scroll work or, if you will, a ram's head. The tail is made in this fashion so as to give the appearance of coming to a point when viewed from either side. Leave enough thickness to this area to give it strength for actual use. If you actually brought the tail to a point, there wouldn't be enough difference in thickness between the tail of the sea horse and the blade. The effect we are trying to create would be lost.

Now exchange your sanding drum for a sanding disc as shown in Fig. 7-12 and start rounding off the areas in between the stomach and the tail and in between the upper part of the tail and the lower part where it curves into the scroll. As you do this, change back to

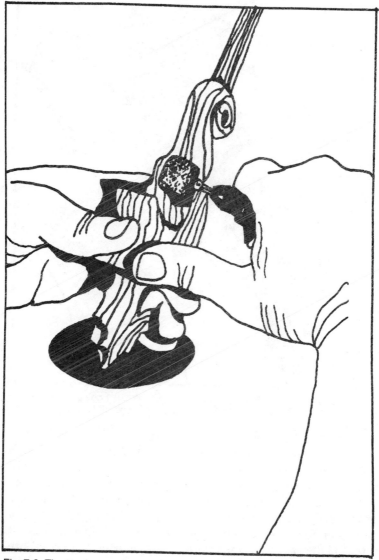

Fig. 7-8. The two large spines are not brought out to a point, but left in a straight line across the width of the sea horse. Sanding drum is being used to start cutting out the area in between the smaller spines. Don't try to bring them out to a point at this time.

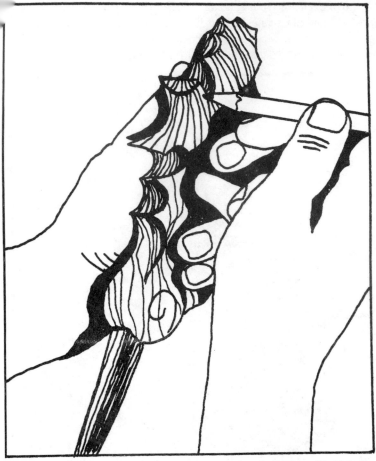

Fig. 7-9. Line from top of the fin should curve out into the body and back in the bottom of the fin. The back of the tail has been rounded off to a rough stage.

your sanding drum and round off the stomach. You will want to change from disc to the drum several times and not try to finish with one completely before changing to the other. In Fig. 7-12 we have rounded off the front of the tail, the stomach and the scroll at the bottom of the tail. You will notice the sanding disc I am using has a sanding surface on both sides. This was made by gluing two pieces of sandpaper together, letting them dry under a weight to prevent curling of the paper, and then cutting out a circle of the desired size with scissors.

In working down the areas between the spines, use a cone-shaped grinding stone as illustrated in Fig. 7-13. As the stone has a tendency to burn the wood if you press very hard, you will want to use care at this point. Turn your Moto-tool down to a low speed. You will use the stone to work down all the areas between the spines on the head, the back and around the neck. You can also use a small *X-acto* knife to cut down the areas between the spines if you desire. Use the knife to make a sharp line around the scroll work on the tail.

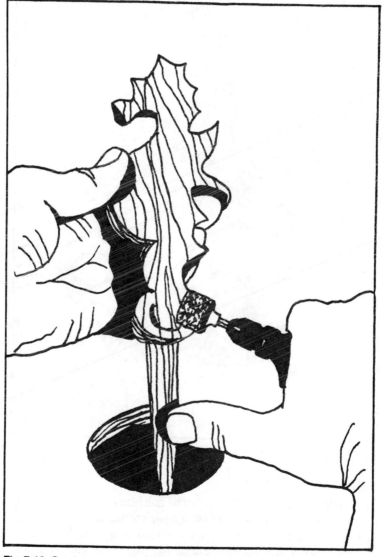

Fig. 7-10. Cut down each side of the tail, ending your cut on the upsweep at the front.

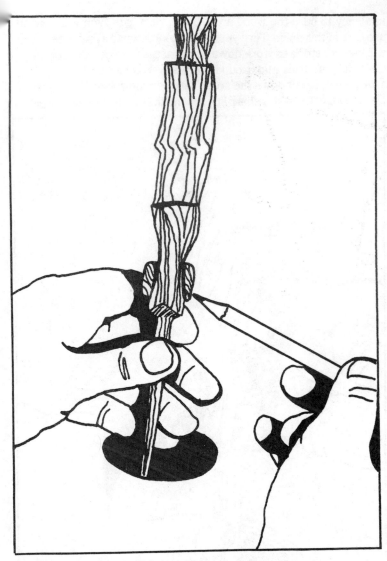

Fig. 7-11. Back view of tail during roughing-in stage.

FINISHING THE PROJECT

Your rough carving should now be complete. Once again it is up to your thumb and a piece of sandpaper to complete the project. Follow the same procedure you used on your free-form letter opener. Start with a #80 grade of garnet paper and work your way down until you wind up with the #600 wet or dry paper. Use the #80 grade to complete sanding between the spines and bring them almost to a point. You can roll up a piece of sandpaper or wrap it around a short length of dowel rod for this purpose. Be sure you don't sand too much in one place. Work the blade down with a sanding block as you did before. Throughout your carving, you

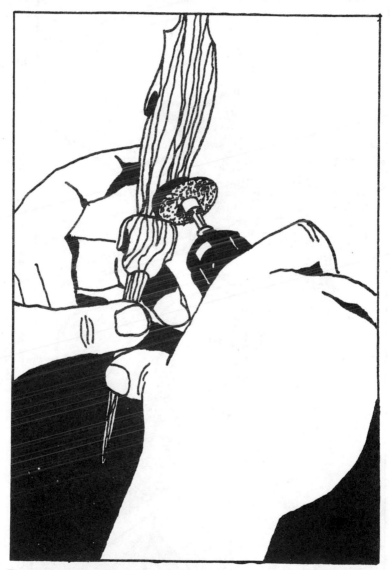

Fig. 7-12. Use a sanding disc to smooth out areas between the tail and the body, and the tail and the "scroll work" portion of the tail.

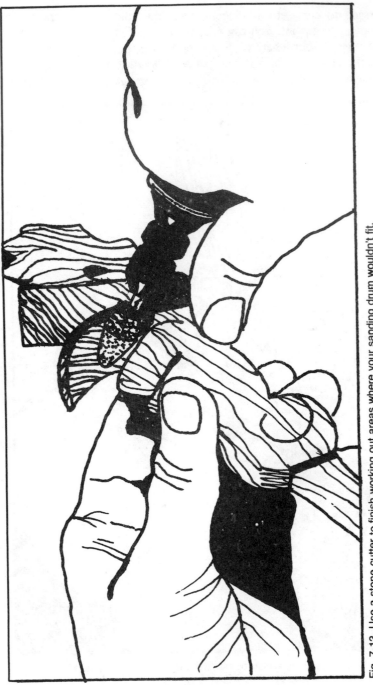

Fig. 7-13. Use a stone cutter to finish working out areas where your sanding drum wouldn't fit.

should refer back fo Fig. 7-1 to keep the lines of the spines and the fin running in the desired manner.

As you work down the blade to arrive at a sharp edge when you reach a fine grade sandpaper, you will want to work down the areas between the spines and bring them to a sharp point in the same manner. If you bring them to a sharp point with a rough grade of sandpaper, they will be reduced in size as you continue working them down to get them smooth. This is a common error in this as well as other carving projects. Another common error is to stop sanding before your project is perfectly smooth. Generally speaking, if your project has a white look to it, you have not sanded it enough. When you really get down to the point where it is smooth, it will lose that white look and the grain of the wood will stand out in color. The white look will be replaced by a shiny look.

As some birch has an interesting grain pattern in it, a good finish for your letter opener will be Johnson's paste wax. Use plenty of wax and rub it in until the wood is thoroughly saturated. Let it dry and then buff it down until you obtain a good shine. This may be repeated several times so as to afford good protection from normal usage. You now have a letter opener which would cost you at least $25 in any gift shop.

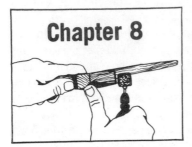

Chapter 8

Project 3— Sperm Whale Wall Plaque

Our next project will be what might be called a scrimshaw style sperm whale plaque. Sailors of long ago had a number of hobbies to keep them occupied on long voyages and during the times they were in home port waiting for their next trip out to sea. Many of these hobbies turned out to be real works of art. They made dolls, ships-in-bottles, jewelry carved from whales' teeth and whales carved from ivory or bone. Such art work has always fascinated me. Much of it was very crude, but there was always some which turned out to be works of art in a very real sense. The whale plaques were especially intriguing as they were something I could carve and display in my home for all to see and admire. Virtually every gift shop or mail order house which deals in this sort of item will offer a plaque of a sperm whale. Almost without fail, these plaques have been turned out by the thousands on a lathe and cannot have the detail of the hand-carved item.

The designs included here were developed by studying the carvings and drawings of the past and combining those with what the whale actually looks like. As ivory is a little costly for most of us to use, we will carve our whales from white pine and paint them white to resemble the real thing. As we are not interested in using a wood which has any particular grain pattern, white pine will be ideal to use because of its ease in carving.

CUTTING METHODS

Figure 8-1 is the photograph of our finished whale. You will notice the photograph was taken before the whale was painted.

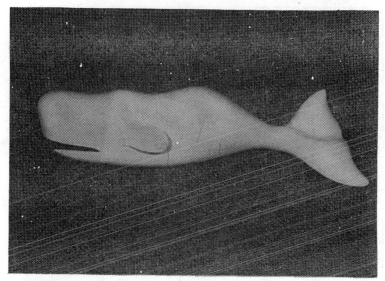

Fig. 8-1. Finished sperm whale.

Figure 8-2 is our scale drawing. When drawing around your pattern on your piece of wood, be sure to draw in the flipper and the line which runs from the body back to the flukes. Again, our material is 1-inch white pine stock. There are three places in which you can start your carving with your sanding drum. In Figure 8-3, the area between the nose and the first hump has been hollowed out, the area between the first and second hump is ready, and the area around the flipper has been worked down. We are working on the tail. Use your sanding drum and make sure you follow the line you have drawn in from the body back to the flukes. As you cut down the top of the flukes, it should curve up into the line you have drawn in and not be a straight, right angle cut. This is the reason for using the sanding drum in the manner indicated.

Figure 8-4 shows the method used in cutting around the flipper. This will be a straight cut around the line drawn, so you will use the edge of your sanding drum. This project, as all others, must be worked on as a whole, and you must be careful not to work the wood down too far all at once in any one spot. This is especially true as you start narrowing down the body where it meets the flukes. In Fig. 8-5, the pencil is pointed towards the line which must be carried up into the body. If you worked either the top or bottom of the flukes, or the body, down too far at once, you would have difficulty in maintaining the line in a graceful curve from flukes to body. Refer back to Fig.

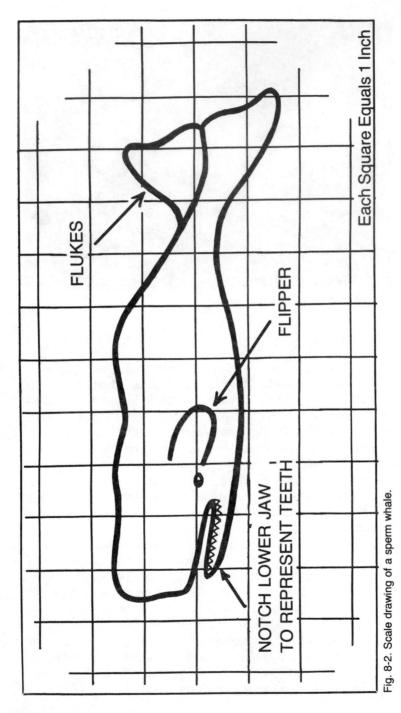

FLUKES

FLIPPER

NOTCH LOWER JAW
TO REPRESENT TEETH

Each Square Equals 1 Inch

Fig. 8-2. Scale drawing of a sperm whale.

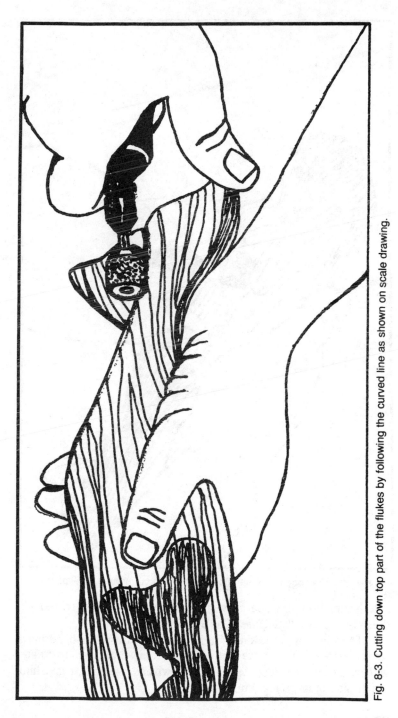

Fig. 8-3. Cutting down top part of the flukes by following the curved line as shown on scale drawing.

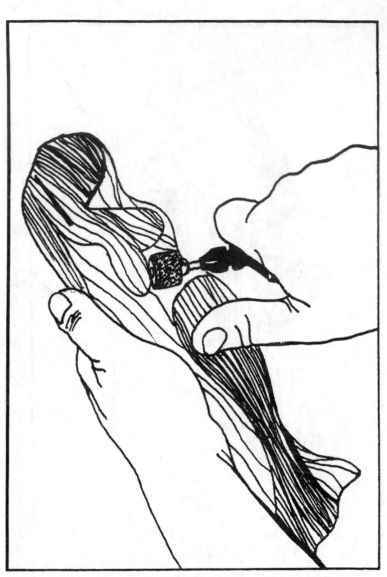

Fig. 8-4. Use the edge of the sanding drum to cut out around the flipper.

8-1. Notice how this line curves up to a sharp edge even though there is a different thickness to this line throughout.

The sperm whale is kind of lumpy looking with a large head and a small under-jaw. This is the kind of impression we will want to create with our finished carving. As with all our whales, we want to give him the illusion of large gracefulness.

WORKING ON THE FLUKES

Going back to Fig. 8-4, notice how the hollow between the second and third hump has been worked down further than the first, and the area between the body and the flukes further yet. This is the overall line we want to follow throughout the carving. Notice, also,

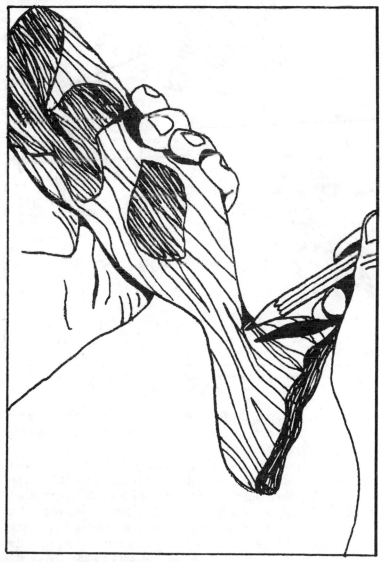

Fig. 8-5. The line between the top and bottom part of the flukes should be carried as a ridge throughout the narrowing down process of the body. Pencil is pointed to this area.

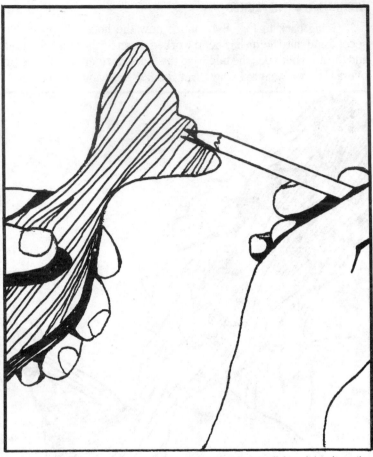

Fig. 8-6. This cut is made on the top and back side of the flukes. It is where the flukes start to curve out away from the plaque.

that the bottom part of the flukes has not yet been touched. We will make the bottom part of the flukes stick out from the plaque to further the three-dimensional effect.

Now refer to Fig. 8-6. Make a shallow cut with your sanding drum as shown on the back side of the upper part of the flukes. This is where the flukes start to curve out away from the plaque itself. Now turn the whale back over and start sanding the front of the lower part of the flukes as shown in Fig. 8-7. As you do this, continue to sand down the area between the body and the flukes until the desired thickness is reached and is one smooth line. Work the bottom part of the flukes down to about the thickness shown. Figure 8-7 also shows how we have left a ridge between the bottom and top part of the flukes and how it curves from the back part of the flukes up into the body.

Now turn the whale back over again and cut down the back of the bottom part of the flukes as shown in Fig. 8-8. This is the part which will stick out away from the plaque. The lower part of the flukes will want to be about the same thickness as the top part when you are finished, or maybe just a bit thicker to give it a little more strength. Throughout your carving on this area, you should continually work from the bottom to the top part of the flukes, from the front to the back of the body and from the body into the flukes. If you don't, you are likely to wind up with an awkward angle between the flukes and the body, or between the top and bottom part of the flukes.

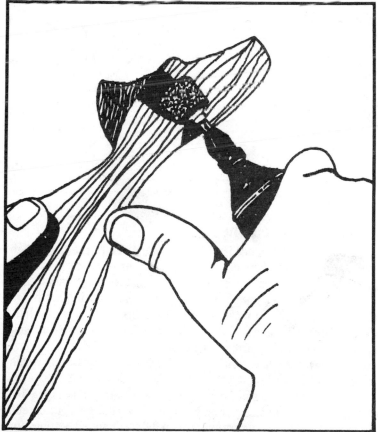

Fig. 8-7. Sand down the lower fluke, making sure the ridge between top and bottom is still maintained throughout. Lower part of the fluke should be cut down to about half the thickness of your piece of material.

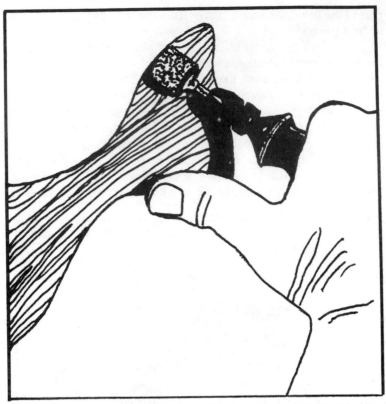

Fig. 8-8. Cut down back side of the lower fluke to approximate thickness of the upper fluke.

SANDING AND UNDERCUTTING

In Fig. 8-9 the pencil is pointed toward one of the three high spots on your whale. The nose and lower jaw have been rounded off and the dark spots showing in Fig. 8-9 are the three high spots. This is about as far as you will want to take it down with your rough sanding drum. As you work it down from here, those three high spots will disappear and become slightly rounded as you will not want any flat spots on your project. Change to a fine sanding drum and work your whole whale down very carefully to take out any rough areas you might have left with the rough sanding drum.

Now change to a small cutting stone as illustrated in Fig. 8-10. Use this stone to undercut the flipper of the whale. Be very careful not to burn the wood. Experiment with different speed settings for your Moto-tool to find the one which allows you to cut with the stone without burning. If you were trying to undercut this area with a knife,

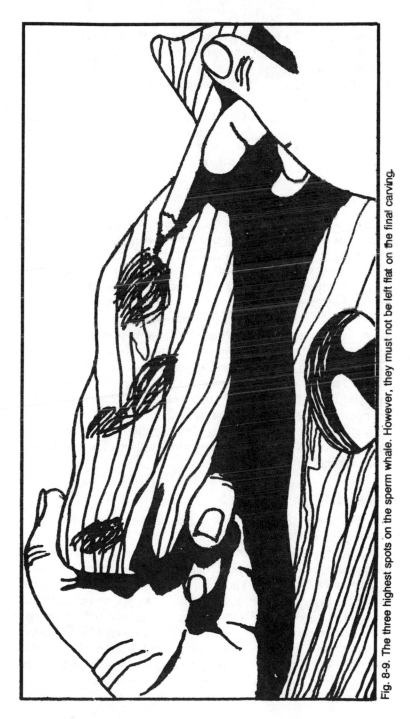

Fig. 8-9. The three highest spots on the sperm whale. However, they must not be left flat on the final carving.

you would find if a tedious job, whereas with the stone it may be accomplished effortlessly and quickly. Now change to a small, fine sandpaper disc to finish sanding the underside of the flipper.

Once again, we are back to using our thumb and sandpaper to finish up the project. Start with a rough grade and work your way down to your final grade of fine wet or dry paper. Use your sanding disc to smooth down the wood inside the mouth. As a final touch, use a small X-acto knife to cut small V-shaped notches in the lower jaw to represent teeth. (Refer back to Fig. 8-1.)

APPLYING PAINT

As we are going to finish our whale in white paint to simulate ivory, it is very important your project be perfectly smooth and free from small lumps and bumps. After it is painted, any small imperfections will stand out very clearly. When you finish sanding it completely, apply a medium coat of thin, white undercoat paint. Let it dry thoroughly; then sand with your finest grade of sandpaper until the project is again perfectly smooth. Paint your whale white with any good brand of spray paint. It might be wise to practice spraying a smooth piece of scrap wood before starting on your whale. Start by spraying around the edges and the underside of the flipper and flukes. Then lay your whale down on a clean sheet of paper and finish spraying the rest of it. Don't try to cover the entire surface with the first coat. After it has dried about an hour, apply a second coat thick enough so the paint will run together slightly to give it a smooth surface. With a little practice, your whale will look like it actually is carved from ivory.

THE PLAQUE

The plaque we will use to mount the whale is very simply made from a piece of 1 × 7-½ × 14-inch white pine. To give it a nautical look, I trimmed the edges with 1/4-inch sisal rope. After sanding down your plaque, use a round, flat-topped steel cutter to make a groove completely around your plaque. Be very careful in doing this as your cutter can very easily get away from you and cut into the edge of the plaque. See Fig. 8-11. Cut your groove in deep enough so that about half of the rope will show. Measure off 7 inches on the bottom edge of the plaque and make a small pencil mark. On each side of the mark, cut in a hole deep enough and big enough to insert the ends of the rope. See Fig. 8-12. An oval steel cutter can best be used for this purpose.

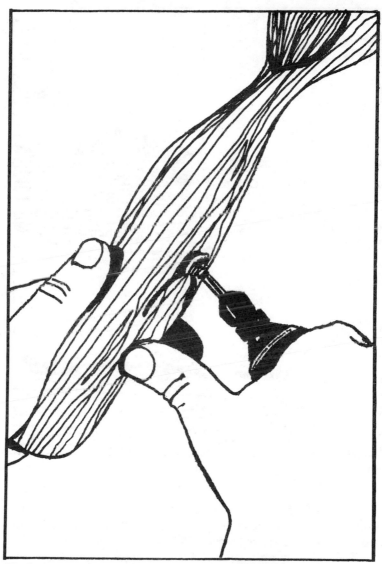

Fig. 8-10. Undercutting the flipper with a small stone cutter.

At this point, the wall plaque should be finished with whatever paint or stain you want. This, of course, depends upon your own desires or on the color of wall you are going to mount it on. The one shown here was stained with a driftwood color. After drying, I applied a coat of Spanish oak wood-graining glaze and wiped it immediately to get the color and effect I wanted. I also gave it

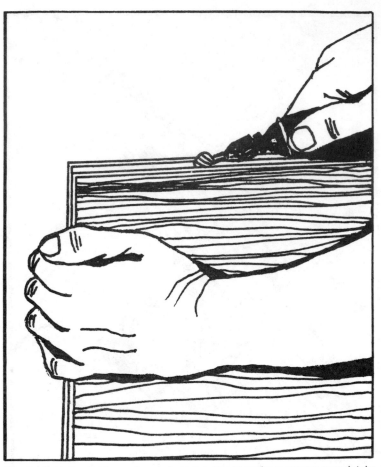

Fig. 8-11. Use a flat-topped, round steel cutter to make a groove completely around your plaque.

several coats of semi-gloss latex varnish. You can experiment around with various colors to get just the shade you want. I have even used a Dutch blue antiquing kit for special purpose.

Let your plaque dry at least 24 hours before starting to work on it again. Cut a piece of ¼-inch sisal rope about 3 or 4 inches longer than necessary to go around your plaque. Insert one end of the rope into the hole you have cut and nail securely in place using a small wire brad. As you drive the brad into the rope, it will all but disappear from sight. See Fig. 8-13. Pull the rope snug as you work your way around the plaque and nail it down about every inch so your rope will lay smooth. Pull the rope tight around the corners and nail as closely as possible on each side of the corner. When you have reached a distance of about 4 l. or 5 inches from going completely around the plaque, stop and measure off the excess rope and cut cleanly. You should have between 1/2 and 1 inch left to push into the hole depending upon how deep you cut it. Fit the end of the rope into the hole before you place any more brads into it. If the rope lays smooth, go ahead and nail it into place. If it doesn't lay smooth, cut off a little more and try it in place again.

Mounting the Plaque

You can use any type hanger you wish to mount it on the wall, but as I have trimmed it in rope, I use a rope hanger. A 13-inch piece

Fig. 8-12. Use an oval steel cutter to make holes in which to inset ends of rope.

Fig. 8-13. Insert end of rope into hole and nail into place with small wire brad.

of rope seems to be the right length for the effect I want. So that the plaque will hang flat against the wall, I cut a groove in the back of the plaque in which to nail my hanger. See Fig. 8-14. I cut the groove at a slight angle so the rope will come out from behind the plaque in a straight line. You can use your own judgment as to how deep or what length groove you want to cut in. Each end of the rope hanger should be wrapped with either plastic or masking tape to help hold the ends of the rope together while nailing to the back of the plaque.

The Nameplate

Your sperm whale plaque is now complete except for mounting the whale onto the plaque itself and attaching a nameplate if so desired. I find epoxy glue very effective for gluing the whale on the plaque. In fact, if you happen to drop it, the wood probably will split before the glue will separate. Figure 8-15 shows the finished sperm whale wall plaque. This particular one happens to be in natural birch with the grain of the wood showing through a plastic spray finish. It is one which I made for a customer who wanted this particular style to go in his den. The nameplate is made of brass which can be obtained from most printing shops, or at least they can order it for you. The plaque itself was stained very lightly with walnut stain so as to show the grain of the white pine stock.

Figure 8-16 shows a humpback whale which has been finished in white paint. I really prefer the whale painted white so as to resemble the ivory used by sailors of long ago. This nameplate is also made of brass. I think it gives it a slightly more elegant look although I have made some with the nameplate in white plastic to match the whale, the lettering being of almost any color you want. Depending upon the color of your plaque, this can also be very attractive. The variations you can come up with go on and on. I made one whale, carved from

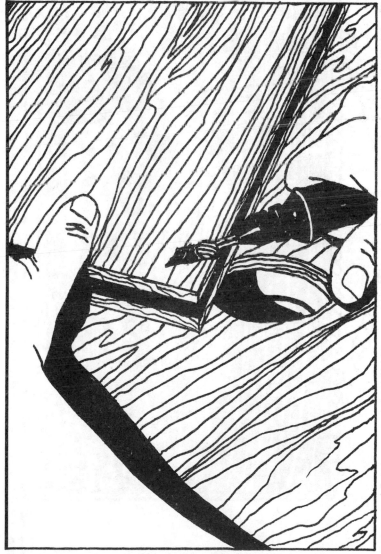

Fig. 8-14. Cutting groove for rope hanger on back side of plaque.

SPERM WHALE

Fig. 8-15. Finished sperm whale plaque. Whale is left in natural birch and the plaque is stained walnut.

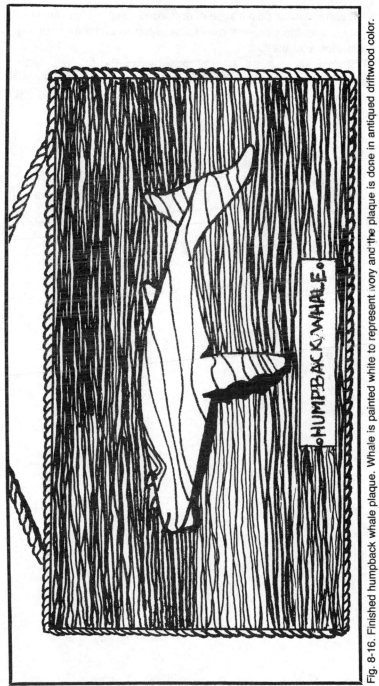

Fig. 8-16. Finished humpback whale plaque. Whale is painted white to represent ivory and the plaque is done in antiqued driftwood color.

walnut and mounted on a plaque of driftwood color, which was very effective. You can use your own imagination to come up with any combination you want.

Since I have shown several drawings of the finished whale plaques in this chapter, I will dispense with the finished plaque for the whales which follow. I will show only the finished whale before it is painted.

Project 4— Right Whale Wall Plaque

Chapter 9

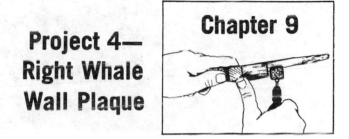

The right whale was hunted almost to extinction during the early days of whaling as it produced more barrels of oil for its size than any other whale. Its most identifying features are a rather lumpy body and a huge mouth. Figure 9-1 is our finished project and Fig. 9-2 is our scale drawing. When drawing your pattern onto the wood, it is very important to draw in the mouth at the proper place. You will be following this line in carving in the main curve of the body. You might notice that on most of my whales, I even draw in the eye so as to get the overall perspective before I get started.

The right whale will be carved in practically the same manner as the sperm whale. Start with your rough sanding drum and work down the top part of the flukes, following the curved line from the body down to the center of the flukes as you did before. Next, cut into the body around the flipper. As your sanding drum will be too large to follow the exact line at the rear of the flipper, finish your rough cut in this area with a round, steel cutter as shown in Fig. 9-3.

WORKING ON THE BODY

In Fig. 9-4 we are cutting down the flipper from the back, following the line of the body. You must use your own judgment as to how far you are going to cut it down. You will want it thin enough to be realistic looking, but not so thin as to break easily.

In Fig. 9-5 we have cut the flipper down from the back and are now starting to narrow down the body where it joins the flukes.

Fig. 9-1. Finished right whale.

Work down the front and back of the flukes in exactly the same manner as you did on the sperm whale. When the flukes have been roughed in, go on to Fig. 9-6. Start rounding off the top of the head and make the cut into the body, following the curve of the mouth as illustrated. When you have roughed in the top of the head and hollowed the body in around the curve of the mouth, move on to the front and lower part of the jaw. Work this whole area down so as to leave as small a flat area as possible along the line of the mouth. Use a stone cutter to cut in the area on the backside of the flipper. Work down the flipper with your stone and your round sanding disc, making sure there are no sanding marks left where the flipper connects to the body.

CUTTING IN THE MOUTH

You should now be ready to cut in the mouth, which is the principal identifying feature of the right whale. Since you have sanded off part of your pencil line while rounding off the head, draw it back in, making sure it curves around the front of the head at the proper angle. You will use the same stone cutter to cut out the mouth that you used to cut out the area behind the flipper. With your Moto-tool turned to a low speed, make just a small notch along your pencil line to start with. When you have notched in the mouth sufficiently enough to give you a good line to follow, you can use

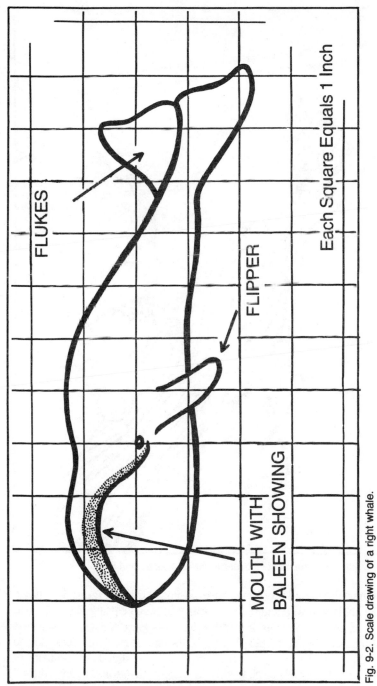

FLUKES

FLIPPER

MOUTH WITH
BALEEN SHOWING

Each Square Equals 1 Inch

Fig. 9-2. Scale drawing of a right whale.

85

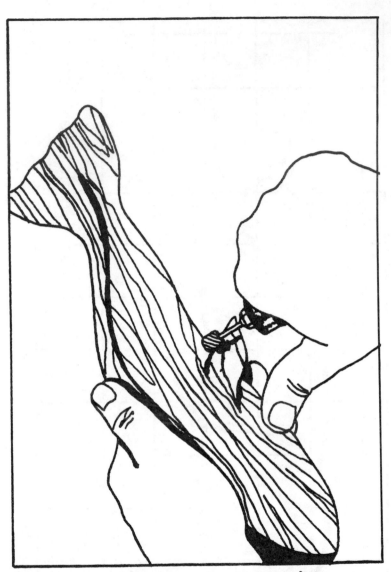

Fig. 9-3. Use a round steel cutter to cut in area behind the flipper.

higher speed and more pressure on your cutter. Figure 9-7 shows the angle you will hold the cutter as you finish cutting in the mouth.

Refer back to Fig. 9-1. Note that the mouth is cut small where it starts back by the flipper. It gets larger as it curves towards the top of the head and finally narrows down ever so slightly at the front of the jaw. As you are cutting with the edge of the stone cutter, you will also want to use upward pressure toward the top of the cutter to widen the mouth. This is what widens the mouth and the edge of the cutter should be kept along the same line at all times. If you have any doubts about the technique used, practice making this cut on a piece of scrap wood until you have it mastered.

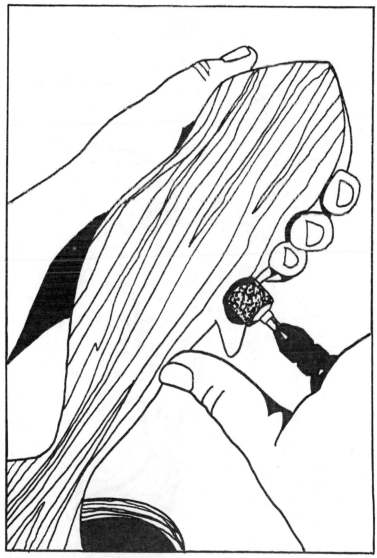

Fig. 9-4. Cut down the flipper from the back with your drum sander, following the line of the body.

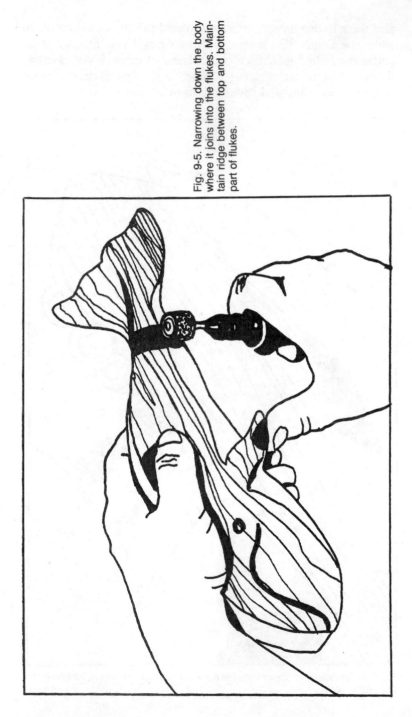

Fig. 9-5. Narrowing down the body where it joins into the flukes. Maintain ridge between top and bottom part of flukes.

REPRESENTING THE BALEEN

When you have the mouth cut out in the proper size, sand the inside of the mouth down slightly by hand. This is one place it will not be necessary to have the wood perfectly smooth. Again refer back to Fig. 9-1. You will notice the inside of the mouth is covered with a pattern of small squares to represent the *baleen* through which the

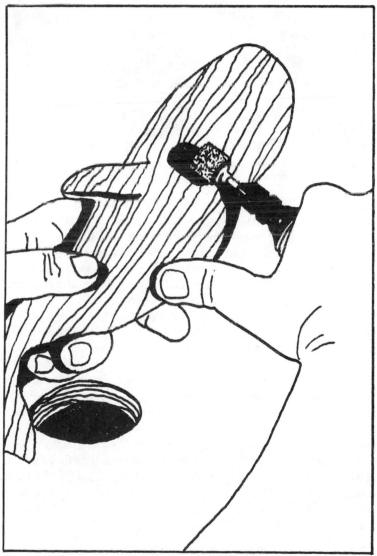

Fig. 9-6. Hollow in the body, following the curve of the mouth.

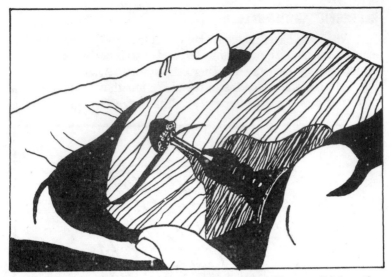

Fig. 9-7. Use a small stone cutter to cut in to mouth, making sure it follows the curve of the body around to the front of the head or jaw area.

whale strains his food. This was accomplished by lightly tapping the point of a #8 common nail into the wood. You will find that most nails do not actually have a sharp point. When the point is tapped lightly against smooth wood, it leaves a square mark. Start at either end of the mouth and make a line of small squares along the entire length of the mouth using this method. Then fill in another line, and another, until the inside of the mouth is completely covered.

It's time for your thumb and sandpaper to get back to work and finish your project off. I might mention at this point that since you are using an undercoat, and then spray painting your whales white, you might be tempted to leave some small sanding marks in your wood as the paint will fill them up. Even though it might do so, I would not recommend getting into the habit of depending on your paint to fill up those small scratches. This is sloppy work and a very bad practice to get into. Remember, the difference between an average and a good project many times depends upon your finish sanding. Finish up your right whale by undercoating, sanding and then applying a flowing coat of white spray paint as before. While your whale is drying, make your wall plaque as described in the previous chapter. If you are making a set which is to be displayed together, try to get the color of the wall plaque as close to the others as possible.

Project 5— Narwhal Wall Plaque

Chapter 10

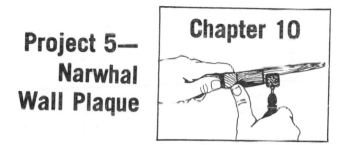

The *narwhal* was a favorite carving of sailors because of its strange and unusual appearance. The long, curved tusk was a prized trophy and would bring a good price. At one time, tusks were sold as the horn of the fabled unicorn. Actually this horn is not a horn at all, but one of two tusks, or teeth, which grow from the mouth of the narwhal. The older the narwhal, the longer the tusk. I don't think anyone is quite sure just what nature had in mind for this tusk. Depending on what natural science book you read, you will get a different explanation.

WORKING DOWN THE TUSK

Figure 10-1 is your finished narwhal and Fig. 10-2 is your scale drawing. When cutting the narwhal out of your wood, leave the tusk a

Fig. 10-1. Finished narwhal.

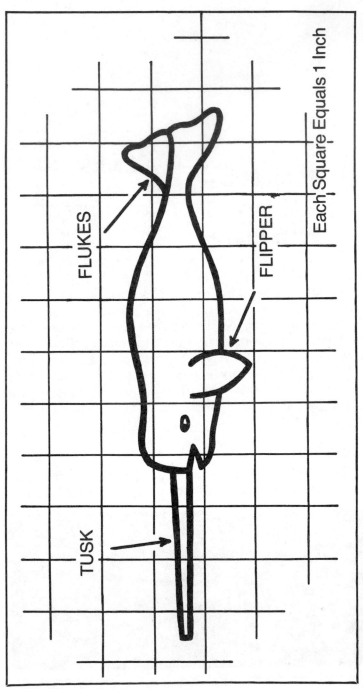

FLUKES

FLIPPER

Each Square Equals 1 Inch

TUSK

Fig. 10-2. Scale drawing of a narwhal.

little larger than you would normally cut out a pattern. This will give you plenty of leeway in working down the tusk in a straight line and to a fairly sharp point. Start your carving by working down the tusk first. Use the same method you used in working down the blade on your letter opener. In Fig. 10-3 we have cut the tusk down and are using the coarse sanding drum to make a right angle cut where it joins the head. Notice that we have not attempted to bring it down to size or a point at this time. This should be done by hand, using a sanding block so as to make it as straight as possible.

The narwhal is carved in exactly the same manner as the others. In Fig. 10-4 we have worked down the top of the flukes, cut in around the flipper and are in the process of working down the urea between the head and the body. Note that this area is directly above and in line with the flipper. In Fig. 10-5 we have roughed out the rest of the body, the lower and back part of the flukes. The pencil is pointed toward the highest spot on the carving, that of the middle of the body. Work down the narwhal with sandpaper exactly the same as the others, leaving the tusk until last. As the tusk will become fairly thin and fragile when it is completely worked down to size and to a point, it is better to leave it until the rest of the narwhal has been worked down to a fine finish. You wouldn't want to take a chance on breaking it while working on another part of the project.

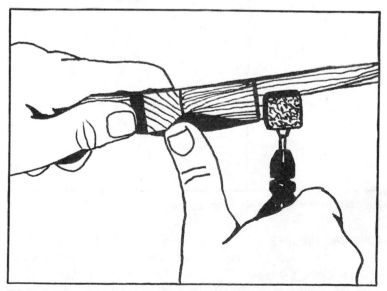

Fig. 10-3. After working down the tusk, make a right angle cut where it joins the head.

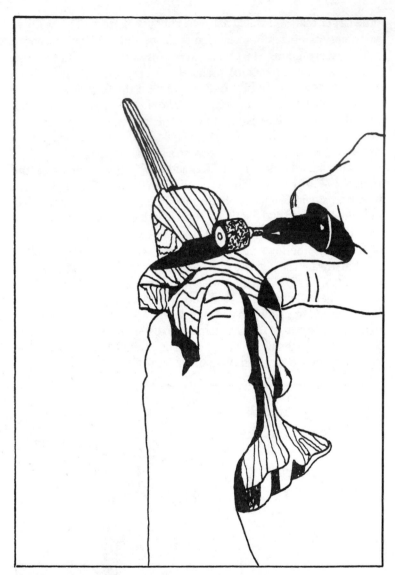

Fig. 10-4. Hollow out the body directly above the flipper.

FINISHING TOUCHES

When the tusk has been worked down to size and sanded, a series of diagonal cuts should be made along the entire length to give it the appearance of being a curved tusk. This is done with a stone cutting disc as shown in Fig. 10-6. Draw in the lines you want to cut,

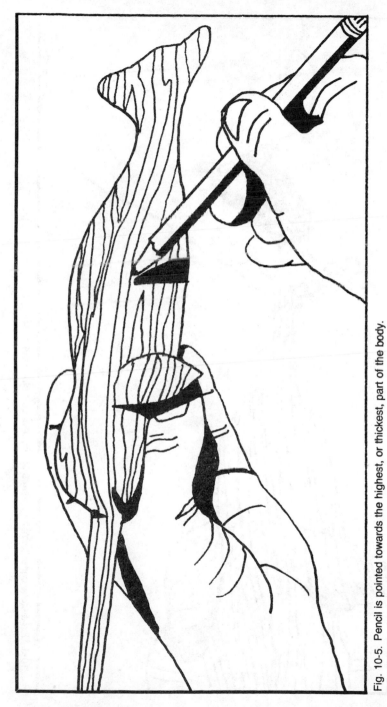

Fig. 10-5. Pencil is pointed towards the highest, or thickest, part of the body.

Fig. 10-6. Use a stone cutter to make a series of diagonal cuts along the tusk.

with pencil, before starting your actual cutting. After making the series of cuts with the stone disc, fold a piece of fine sandpaper in half and widen the grooves just slightly by hand. They should be wide and deep enough to show up good after the narwhal is painted.

Finish up your narwhal by painting with undercoat. Then spray paint after it has been sanded down again. Mount the narwhal on your wall plaque in the same manner as the others.

You will notice the instructions are getting less and less as we progress from one whale to the next. As the basic shape is treated the same in all of them, I am only mentioning a few small differences in each.

Chapter 11

Project 6— Humpback Whale Wall Plaque

The humpback whale makes a very interesting carving. He is one of the more graceful and streamlined looking whales in the water and is easily recognizable by his long flippers and several rows of warlike protuberances around his jaw. Figure 11-1 is your finished humpback whale and Fig. 11-2 is your scale drawing. Carving in a double row of warts around the jaw would be a tremendous job, so we will make two warts on the top of his nose to represent this feature. Remember, your carvings are designed to show the out-

Fig. 11-1. Finished humpback whale.

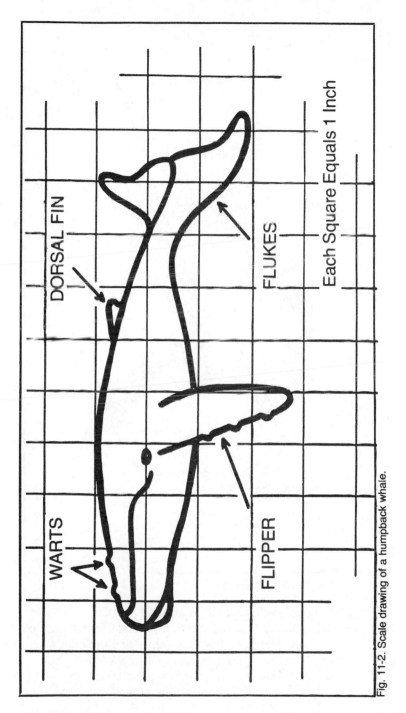

DORSAL FIN

FLUKES

Each Square Equals 1 Inch

WARTS

FLIPPER

Fig. 11-2. Scale drawing of a humpback whale.

99

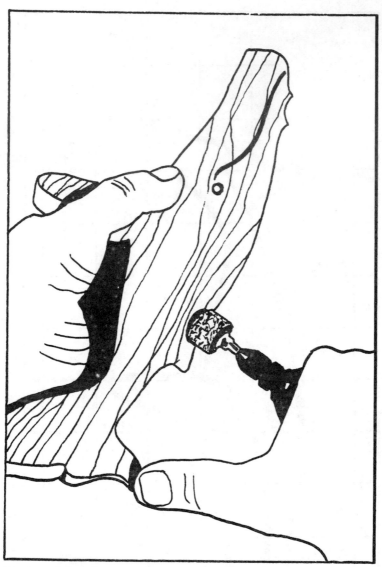

Fig. 11-3. Cutting down the dorsal fin.

standing features of each whale in what could be called scrimshaw style. You will also notice a large protuberance on the underside of the jaw. The other difference from this whale and the others you have carved is the addition of a dorsal fin on the back of the whale.

In Fig. 11-3 we have started our carving with the rough sanding drum by working down the flukes, cutting around the flipper and cutting down the dorsal fin. The dorsal fin should be fairly thin and should stick up from the body. Refer back to Fig. 11-1 and you will notice the protuberance on the underside of the jaw is cut the same way except that it is rounded instead of flat. The same thing applies to the two warts on the top of the nose.

The flipper of the humpback whale should have a slight curve to it. Figure 11-4 gives you a good front view of the amount of curve which should be used. You will want to use a larger stone cutter to undercut the flipper of the humpback than you used on the other whales. In Fig. 11-5 we are using a cone-shaped stone cutter to work down the forward edge of the flipper. This drawing also provides a good view of the two warts on the nose and the larger protuberance

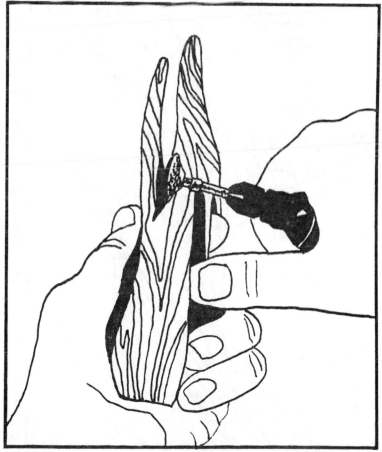

Fig. 11-4. Use stone cutter to undercut the flipper. It should have a small amount of curve as shown.

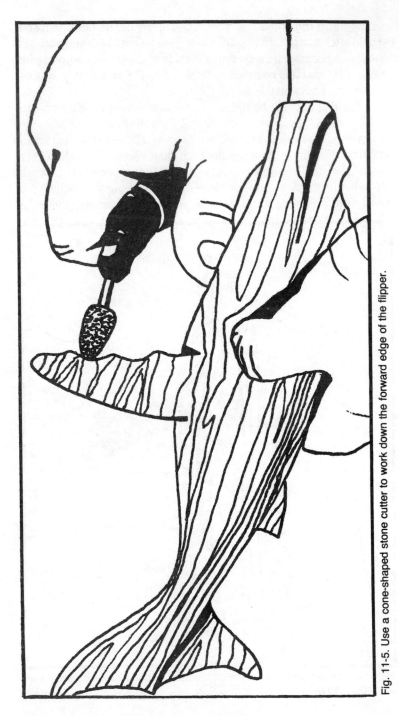

Fig. 11-5. Use a cone-shaped stone cutter to work down the forward edge of the flipper.

on the underside of the jaw. These should be rounded as opposed to the flat shape of the dorsal fin. The line of the mouth should be cut in the same manner as that of the right whale, except not to such an extreme. Use just the edge of your cutter with only a slight upward pressure.

Finish sanding your humpback whale as you did the others and paint white. I should mention here that extra caution should be exercised when working down the flipper because it is so long, and easy to break off if you use too much pressure against it. Mount your humpback whale on the plaque the same as the others.

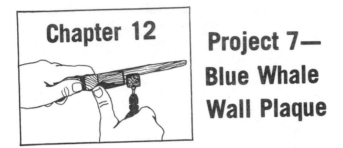

Chapter 12

Project 7—
Blue Whale
Wall Plaque

By now, you should be totally familiar with the steps in carving out your whales and the blue whale should be carved out following the techniques you used on the others. Figure 12-1 is your finished whale and Fig. 12-2 is your scale drawing. The hump on the head of the blue whale is actually the blowhole and should be carved in a round shape like the warts on the humpback. The mouth of the blue

Fig. 12-1. Finished blue whale.

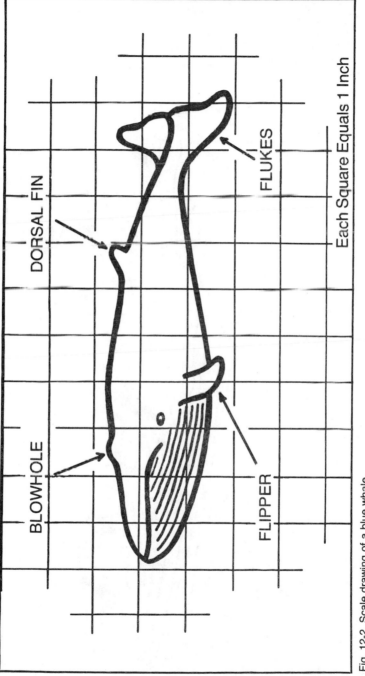

Fig. 12-2. Scale drawing of a blue whale.

DORSAL FIN

FLUKES

BLOWHOLE

FLIPPER

Each Square Equals 1 Inch

105

Fig. 12-3. Pencil is pointed to thickest area of body.

whale will be a cross between the right whale and the humpback whale. It should be cut in far enough so it will give the impression of being slightly open. Figure 12-3 shows your rough carving with the pencil pointed towards the highest area, which is right above the flipper.

The most distinguishing features of the blue whale will be the blowhole on the top of the head and the grooves carved in on the lower side of the jaw. These should be cut in with a small stone cutter and should be done after the whale is almost completely sanded. Draw your lines in with pencil before starting to make your grooves. Refer back to Fig. 12-1. The grooves should be an equal space apart and should end at an equal distance below the mouth. Use a very light touch in starting out the grooves. Cutting these in a crooked line will give a very poor appearance to your finished whale. Finish up your blue whale and mount it on your plaque in the same manner as the others.

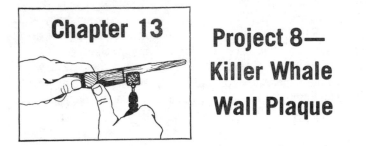

Chapter 13

Project 8—
Killer Whale
Wall Plaque

Figure 13-1 is your finished whale and Fig. 13-2 is your scale drawing. The most distinguishing feature of the killer whale is the high dorsal fin on the back. Otherwise, he is very sleek and stream-lined in appearance. There is no need to go into any of the processes in the carving of this whale as he should be the simplest of all the whales which make up your set. Just keep referring back to Fig. 13-1 as you work and you will have no trouble. The one thing you want to be careful of is leaving too much of a flat spot down the length of the body. Otherwise, flipper, flukes and dorsal fin are carved out in the same manner as the others.

Now that you have finished your series of whale wall plaques, you can readily see how easily this was accomplished by using the Moto-tool. The only place you might want to have used a knife was to help in undercutting the flipper. Even then, almost all this can be done by careful use of your stone cutters and sanding discs. As an exercise in using your knife, cut out the easiest whale, which would be the killer whale, and rough out the complete project with an *X-acto* or similar knife. Notice how careful you will have to be to cut in the proper direction so as not to cut into the grain of the wood. You will find it takes a lot more practice and skill in whittling away the wood to get it as smooth as you can with the Moto-tool.

This might be a good place to mention that a rubber thumb and finger is a most useful implement to use, either when using a knife or when sanding by hand. You will find that if you are doing a lot of hand

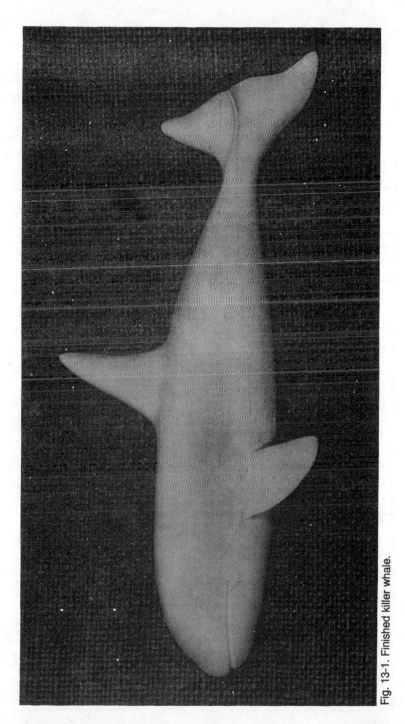

Fig. 13-1. Finished killer whale.

109

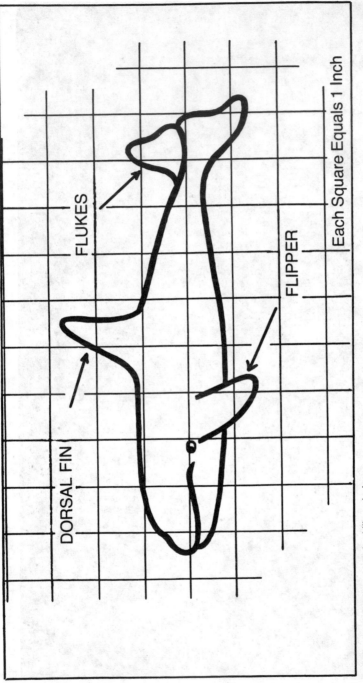

FLUKES

DORSAL FIN

FLIPPER

Each Square Equals 1 Inch

Fig. 13-2. Scale drawing of a killer whale.

sanding with a very rough grade of sandpaper, you will be sanding down your fingers as much as you are the wood. If you are going to practice carving with a knife, it will keep you from getting those small slices in the end of your thumb and fingers, which is bound to happen. The rubber thumb and finger may be purchased from most office supply stores. If you have trouble in finding them, a piece of masking tape wrapped around your thumb will serve the purpose very well.

Chapter 14

Project 9—
Inletting

Earlier in the book we mentioned inletting as just one of the ways in which carving can be used in a practical manner. A very handsome desk set can be made by inletting a pocket calculator into a piece of wood. Figure 14-1 is an illustration of what can be done by fitting a pocket calculator into a block of wood and adding several pen holders to complete your set. There is no particular pattern to use as it depends on what size calculator you might want. In Fig. 14-2 a block of 1-inch walnut has been sanded down and cut to a size which will leave an appropriate border around the calculator. The back side of the calculator I am using is smaller than the face, and this is the portion I want to inlet. Use a paper pattern to draw around the portion you want to inlet; then copy it off on your block of wood. Some calculators do not have this lip, so you will want to set the calculator into the wood at a depth of your own choice. If you are going to set some pen holders into your set, leave room for them at the top of your block of wood.

Using a paper pattern to draw around on your block of wood is a much more efficient method than trying to draw around your calculator. This way you can keep cutting down your paper pattern with scissors until you have exactly the right size pattern before drawing it off on your wood.

INLETTING THE CALCULATOR

When you have the area you want to inlet correctly marked off, use a flat-topped, round steel cutter to start your inletting. See Fig.

14-3. Make your cut slightly on the inside of the line you have drawn. Cut completely around the line you have drawn and just deep enough to give you a good line to work with. Don't try to make the corners of your cut too sharp with your round cutter at this time.

You now have the choice of using your Moto-tool to grind out the area you want to inlet or of using a small *X-acto* chisel. In Fig.

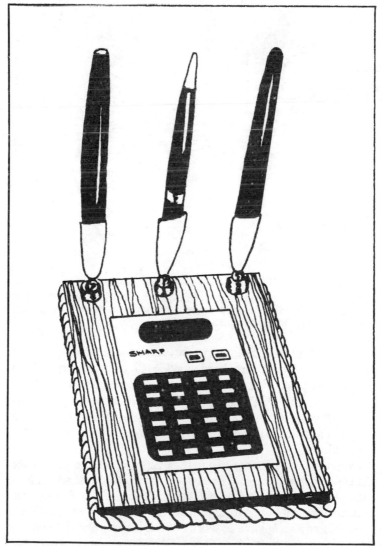

Fig. 14-1. Deck set made by inletting bottom side of a pocket calculator into a block of walnut and adding pen holders.

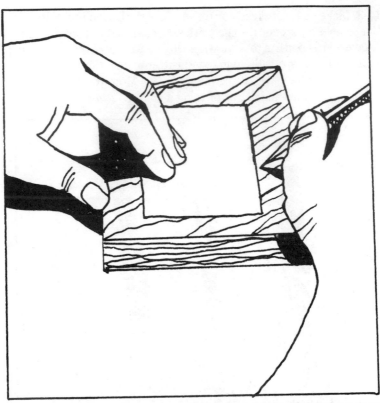

Fig. 14-2. After making a paper pattern of the bottom side of your calculator, draw around the pattern on your block of wood. This method is much more efficient than trying to draw around the calculator itself.

14-4 I am using the chisel to cut out the area in which to fit my calculator. Walnut is a fairly hard wood, but it chips very easily and you can work down a very level area using this method. You will also notice in Fig. 14-4 that I have made a groove around my block of wood. I am going to trim it with rope in the same manner as the whale plaques. The holes to insert the ends of the rope are made at the top of the set.

When you are getting close to the depth you want to insert your calculator, stop and carefully sand down the inletted area with a #50 grade of sandpaper, keeping it level at all times. Try fitting your calculator into this area to see how you are progressing. Use a sharp-pointed *X-acto* knife to work out the corners and to keep the edges of your cut sharp. If the area is not deep enough, start over again and keep working in this manner until your calculator almost is

114

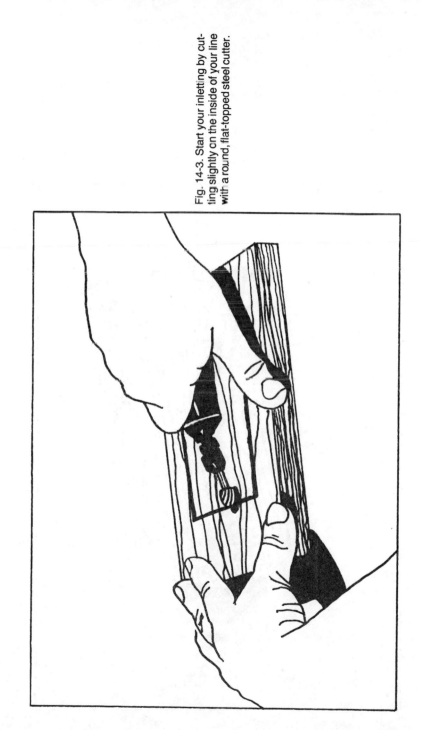

Fig. 14-3. Start your inletting by cutting slightly on the inside of your line with a round, flat-topped steel cutter.

115.

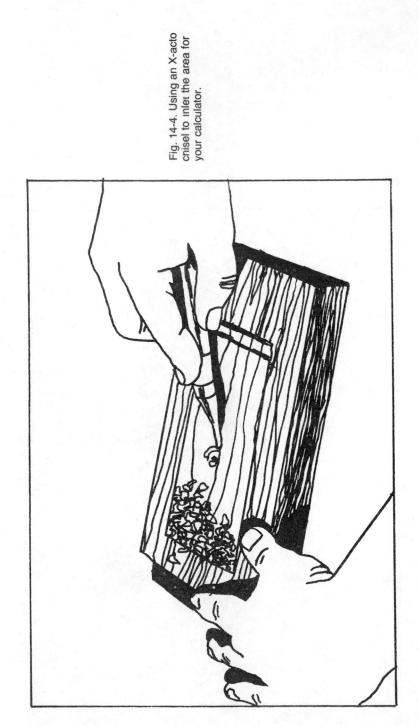

Fig. 14-4. Using an X-acto chisel to inlet the area for your calculator.

at the right depth. Then start sanding your inletted area down until it is the right depth. Mark off the holes you want for your pen holders and drill out the holes of the proper size for the attaching screws. Be sure to countersink the underside for the nuts to fit into. Sand your whole project down until it is glassy smooth and wax with Johnson's paste wax. This project gives you a lot of leeway. You may want to use a small calculator as I did, or you may want to use a larger, print-out calculator. You can put in as many pen holders as you have room for, according to your own personal needs.

INLETTING AN OVAL CAMEO

This is a fairly simple inletting project, all the edges being straight and square. Another project to give you practice in inletting is to make a letter opener, inletting an oval cameo. The cameo as shown in Fig. 14-5 is made of plastic and contains two white geese on a black background. This and many other cameos or stones suitable for inletting may be purchased from Grieger's, 990 South Arroyo Parkway, Pasadena, California 91109. Figure 14-6 is your scale drawing and your material is 1-inch walnut stock.

As our first project was making letter openers, we won't need to go very far into the particulars of the carving except for the inletting. Work your letter opener down with your rough sanding drum until you get about to the stage shown in Fig. 14-7. In Fig. 14-8

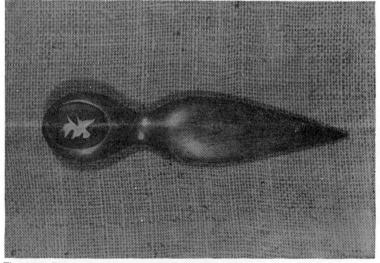

Fig. 14-5. Finished letter opener with inletted cameo.

117

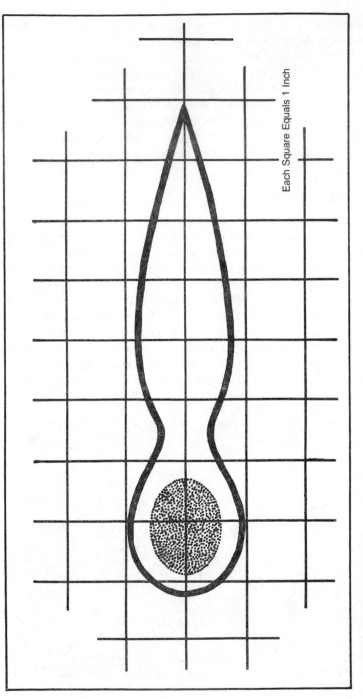

Each Square Equals 1 Inch

Fig. 14-6. Scale drawing of a letter opener.

118

we are starting to work the blade down by hand with a sanding block, using a #50 grade of sandpaper. Because the blade of this letter opener is pretty wide, it is much easier to get the blade straight by working it down by hand from this point on. When you have the blade

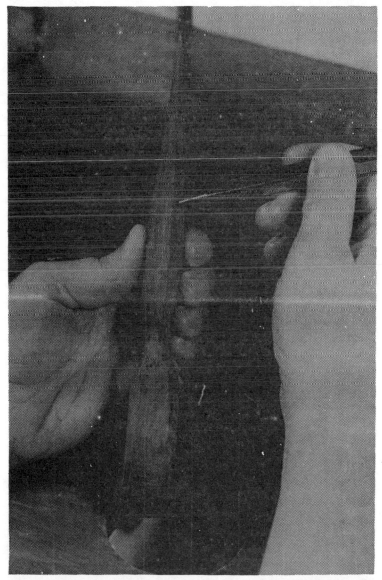

Fig. 14-7. Work blade down to approximately the thickness shown with drum sander.

worked down pretty much to shape, start rounding off the top of the handle. Bring it down pretty much to a finished stage. Make a paper pattern of the cameo or other object you want to inlet into the handle and then draw around your pattern onto the wood. You must remember that when you are drawing around an object, your pencil line is going to be slightly larger than the pattern you are drawing around.

Using your round, flat-topped steel cutter, make your initial cut on the inside of your pencil line. Again, you can use an oval cutter with your Moto-tool or a small chisel to cut out this area. Stop quite often to see how your cameo is fitting into the cut-out area. Now refer to Fig. 14-9. We have pretty much worked down the letter opener to the finished stage and the inletted area is getting pretty

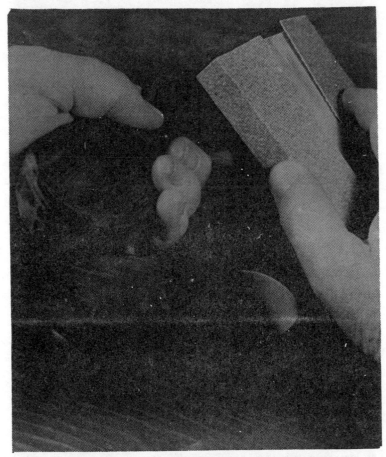

Fig. 14-8. Use sanding block diagonally across blade to keep it straight.

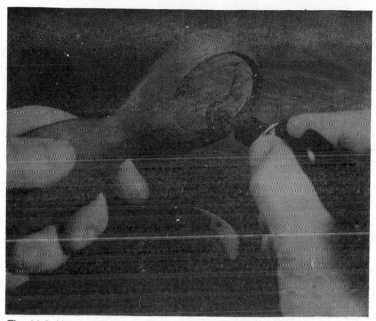

Fig. 14-9. Use small round stone to trim edges of inletted area.

close to size. Now use your Moto-tool with a small, flat stone to finish up. As you can see from the photograph, we are using the small, flat stone to level off the inletted area as well as to round off the sides for the final fit. When you are fitting your cameo or other object into the inletted area to check for size, do not use much pressure. Sooner or later you will have the experience of pushing the cameo in too hard, and then not being able to remove it if your inletted area needs a little more depth to it.

There are any number of ways you can use inletting to decorate an object. A fairly new hobby is putting together black powder gun kits. You can really dress up your gun by inletting a figure into the stock which has been carved from a different color wood. Knife handles, cigarette or jewelry boxes are just a few of the many items which can be dressed up with this process. It would, however, be wise to practice inletting a few objects into a blank piece of wood before starting on an object which would be hard to replace if your fit wasn't correct.

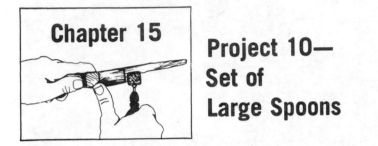

Chapter 15

Project 10— Set of Large Spoons

Almost every gift shop across the country offers a set of some kind of wooden kitchen utensils: spoons, forks, etc. Some are meant only to be decorative and some actually serve a useful purpose. Your Moto-tool is ideal for producing any of these items, and you can make them in any shape or size you desire. This is also an excellent exercise in control and shaping. We will make a set of four different large spoons, starting off with a large mixing or stirring spoon. Figure 15-1 is the photograph of our four finished spoons. Figure 15-2 is the scale drawing and a silhouette view of our first spoon.

If you want your spoons to be usable as well as decorative, you should use a hard wood. All the kitchen utensils shown here are made of walnut. Birch is an ideal wood to use as it is very durable in actual use. Your material should be 1-inch stock of whatever kind of wood you decide to use. I might mention here that if you are going to use walnut use a black felt tip pen to draw around your pattern onto the wood. A pencil mark will not show up very well. Cut out your spoon the same as any other project; that is, cut it just on the outside of your line so that the pen line is still visible after it is cut out.

WORKING DOWN THE SPOON

The first step is to form the bottom part of the spoon from the front to the back. In Fig. 15-3 the bottom part of the spoon has been roughed out from the tip of the spoon to where it starts out onto the handle. The pencil is pointed to the side of the tip, and you will notice the sides have not been taken down at all. You can work down the

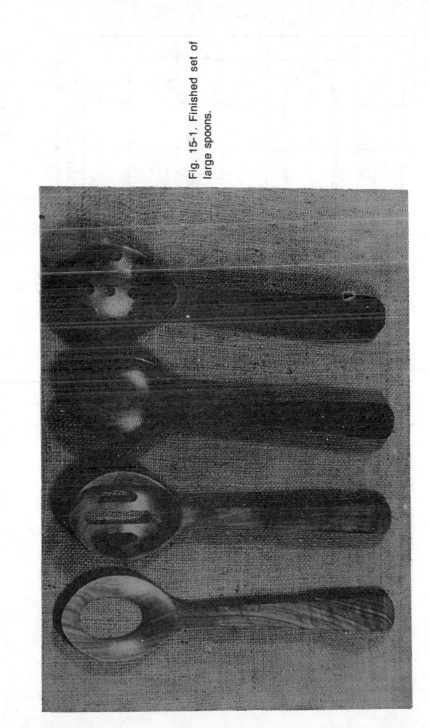

Fig. 15-1. Finished set of large spoons.

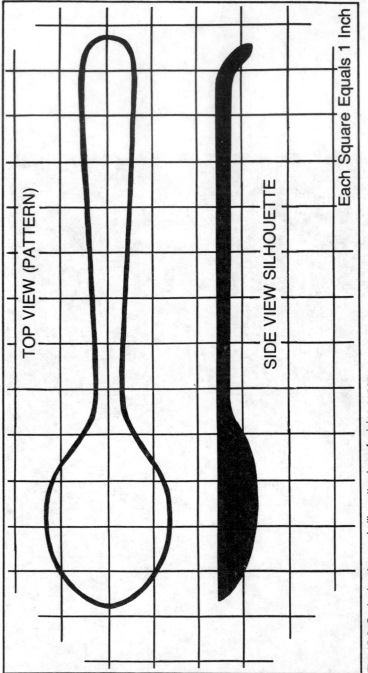

TOP VIEW (PATTERN)

SIDE VIEW SILHOUETTE

Each Square Equals 1 Inch

Fig. 15-2. Scale drawing and silhouette view of mixing spoon.

bottom of the spoon from front to back and the sides at the same time if you desire. However, I have found it a little easier to get the shape of the spoon a little more uniform if I shape the front to back section first. Then I start working down the sides.

In Fig. 15-4 we have started rounding the sides. The idea is to get the bottom of the spoon as round as possible. It would help for you to make an "X" mark on the center of the bottom of the spoon and work towards the "X" from all sides. The tendency is to leave the bottom of the spoon too flat. When you get it pretty well down to shape with your rough sanding drum, start sanding it down by hand with a piece of #50 sandpaper. From there, go to a #80 and then a #100 grade of sandpaper, working it down as smooth as possible so you will have a good bottom surface to work toward from the top.

THE HOLLOWING-OUT PROCESS

When you have the bottom of the spoon worked down to your satisfaction, turn the spoon over and make a pen mark around the outside edge of the top. Use this as a guide when you start hollowing it out. Make this pen line a good distance in from the edge of your spoon. There is no particular measurement in from the edge that this line should be drawn. As you can see from Fig. 15-5, I draw it in far enough so there will be no danger of my working too close to the edge of the spoon as I start the hollowing-out process. Use an oval steel cutter for this work. Start by cutting in all the way around the pen line you have made. When this has been cut in, start cutting out the entire area by a strip at a time. Don't try to cut in too deep in any

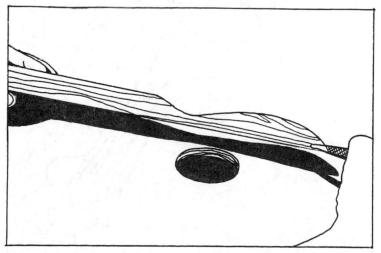

Fig. 15-3. The bottom curve of the spoon should be roughed in first.

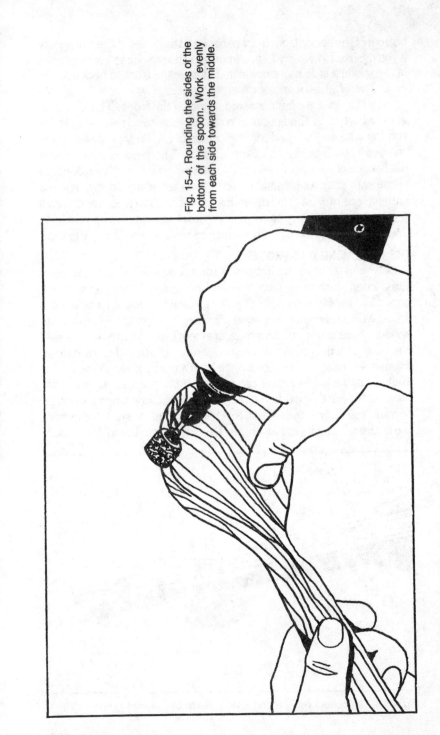

Fig. 15-4. Rounding the sides of the bottom of the spoon. Work evenly from each side towards the middle.

one spot. Rather, keep cutting the wood away a layer at a time, making each cut as uniform as possible. Work from the sides towards the center. This hollowing-out process should not be hurried and, again, remember to be careful not to cut too deep in any one spot.

As you work, keep testing the thickness by holding the area you are working on between your thumb and forefinger. After you have

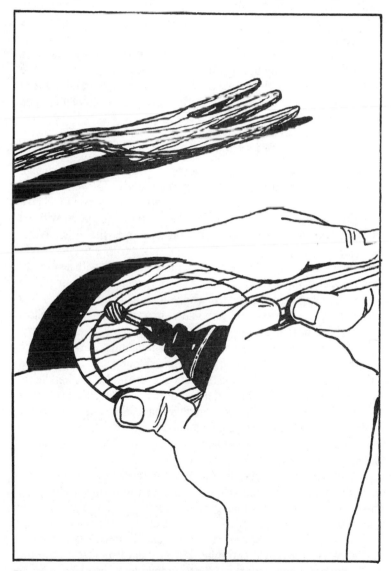

Fig. 15-5. Hollowing out the bowl of the spoon with a steel oval cutter.

done this a few times, you will find you can develop a pretty good feel for the thickness of the wood. When you get down to where you think you are getting fairly close to the thickness you want, stop and start sanding down the hollowed-out area with a piece of #50 sandpaper. I use this grade of sandpaper because it will take the wood down pretty fast and give me an idea if there are any spots which are too high or too low. Remember, you will have to work the entire hollowed-out area down to conform to the lowest spot you have made with your cutter.

At this point, you can see why I have preached the use of a smooth, even cut at all times. Careless use of your cutter will leave you an extremely rough surface to sand down by hand. In this type of work, it is better to use the pencil grip on your Moto-tool after you have made the initial cut around the edge.

SANDING THE STIRRING SPOON

When your spoon is shaped about the way you want it, change to a coarse sanding drum and start working down the wood around the inside of the edge. Use of the sanding drum at this point will give you better control in working up to the edge of the spoon without cutting in too far and running your Moto-tool over the edge. When the edge of the spoon has been brought down to the proper thickness, check to see if the edge of the spoon runs down with a smooth, even thickness to the bottom of the spoon, again using your thumb and forefinger. You can see now why you should start your carving with the bottom of the spoon. It would be pretty hard to try to hollow out the spoon first and then fit the bottom to the hollowed-out part.

Now move on to the handle and start thinning it down from the bottom side. Your silhouette view on Fig. 15-2 gives you a good idea of the thickness to work for and the curve on the end of the handle. In Fig. 15-6 the handle has been thinned down and the curve cut in on the end. We are ready to start sanding by hand. The use of a sanding block on the straight part of the handle allows you to take out any small lumps or bumps which were made during the cutting or the roughing-in process.

When carving out your first spoon, the tendency is to leave too much thickness in the actual spoon, that is, the hollowed-out part. This, of course, is better than getting it too thin. As you are sanding it down by hand and you find the hollowed-out part too thick, don't be afraid to stop, go back to your cutter and take it down another layer. Do this very slowly and carefully. If you think it is just a little too thick, work it down with your #50 sandpaper by hand.

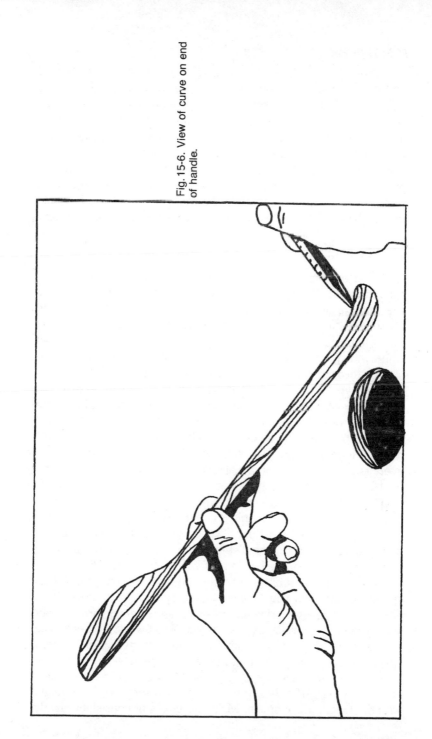

Fig. 15-6. View of curve on end of handle.

APPLYING FINISH

Presuming you have made your spoon from walnut and it is now completely sanded, you will notice that the wood has a light color to it. It's nothing like that pretty walnut furniture you have seen. To obtain the dark walnut color and to bring out the grain pattern, it must have some kind of finish on it. If you are actually going to use your spoon, you will find that it will turn dark with use as the grease from your hands and the food you are stirring are worked into it. I prefer to use Johnson's paste wax to bring out the color and grain to start with. Rub the wax well into the wood and let it dry. It should then be buffed with an electric buffer to remove all the surface wax.

SLOTTED SPOON

Your next spoon will be the large slotted spoon. Use the same pattern you made for your stirring spoon. Figure 15-7 is the drawing showing the slots. When you have your spoon cut out, draw in the areas to be cut out to make your slots. These should be drawn in on the bottom side of the spoon. Using the drill bit which should have come with your Moto-tool, drill several holes, side-by-side, completely through the area. Be very careful to make these holes perfectly vertical through the wood. This is harder to do than you might think and is one reason for drilling the holes from the bottom of the spoon, rather than the top. If the holes are a little crooked, they will come out pretty far off on the top. If the holes were drilled from the top, it would make your slots off-center on the bottom. However, as you will hollow out the spoon from the top, it won't matter if the slots are a little off-center there as that area will be cut away. It won't show up on the finished spoon.

In Fig. 15-8 we have drilled two holes, side-by-side, through each of the slots to be cut out. Two of the slots have been cut out with the use of a small, round steel cutter. In actual practice, these slots should only be roughed in as it will be easier to finish in their shape after you have hollowed out the spoon. Carve out your slotted spoon the same way you did your stirring spoon. It will actually be a little easier than the stirring spoon as you can see down through your slots to check the thickness of the wood as you work. The one thing you have to watch out for is not to let your cutter slip into the areas which you have cut out and ruin the edge of your slots. When you have the hollowed-out area pretty much down to the desired thickness, you can then finish up your slots, making sure they run straight with the length of the spoon. Make the edges of your slots slightly

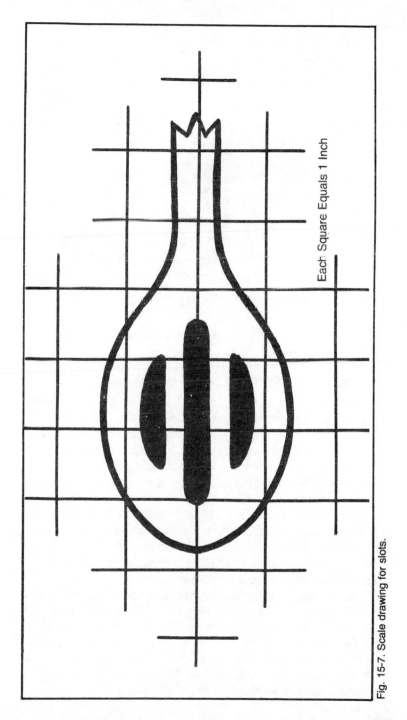

Each Square Equals 1 Inch

Fig. 15-7. Scale drawing for slots.

131

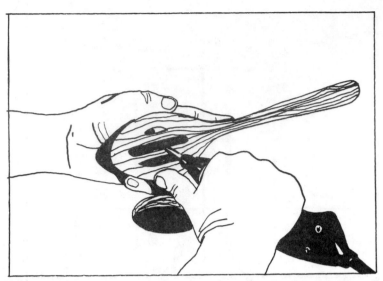

Fig. 15-8. Drill several holes side-by-side: then cut out slotted areas with small steel cutter.

rounded. Finish your slotted spoon in the same manner as you used on your stirring spoon.

SPOON WITH DRAINING HOLES

Your next spoon is the spoon with holes for draining. Figure 15-9 shows the hole pattern. Again, drill your holes from the bottom of the spoon before you start the hollowing-out process. There is another reason for drilling your holes in any such project before you start the actual carving. If you are not extremely careful, the wood will splinter as the drill bit breaks through the wood on the opposite side from which you are drilling. If you were to wait until your spoon was finished and then drilled the holes, there is always the possibility of this happening in an area where it would ruin your project if you had to sand out the splintered area. The draining spoon is carved the same as the others. Remember to be careful not to let your cutter slip into a hole as you are hollowing out.

There is no particular size to make the holes, but you should stay fairly close to the size as shown in Fig. 15-9. As with the slotted spoon, don't try to finish off the holes until you have your spoon down to the desired thickness before hand sanding. Then use your cutter to enlarge the holes. During your finish sanding, you can wrap a piece of sandpaper around a pen, pencil or other round object of an appropriate size and sand the inside of the holes.

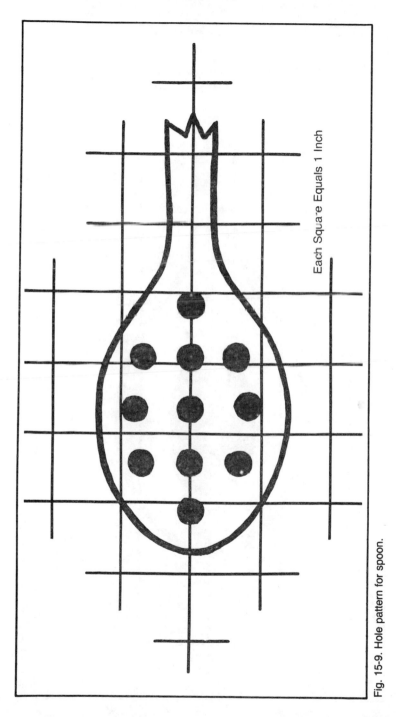

Each Square Equals 1 Inch

Fig. 15-9. Hole pattern for spoon.

133

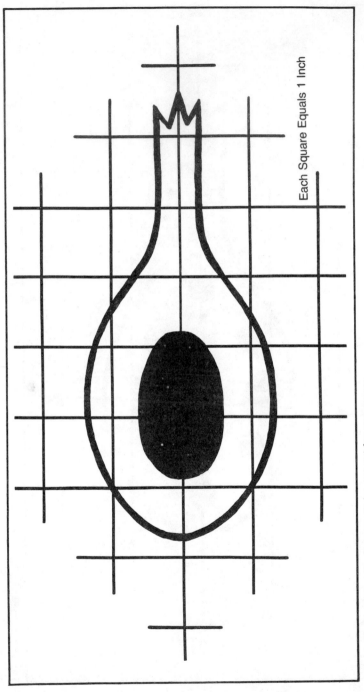

Each Square Equals 1 Inch

Fig. 15-10. Scale drawing for area to be cut out for egg spoon.

EGG SPOON

The last spoon of this set is the large egg spoon. The pattern is the same and Fig. 15-10 is your drawing for the area to be cut out. As this area is fairly large in size, you can drill a hole through the center large enough to fit your jigsaw blade through and cut it out on your saw. Cut it out the same as you would anything else. In this case it would be on the inside of your line, leaving the pen line to show.

The egg spoon will be carved differently from the others in that you will start from the top, using your drum sander instead of a steel cutter. Start working around the inside of the egg spoon to obtain the angle of slope you want. You don't want too steep an angle on it as it would make it look out of proportion. It should slope down at about a 20 degree angle. When you have the top cut in at the angle you want, start working up from the bottom. Be careful not to get it too thin and make sure the edges around the cut-out area are slightly rounded. The spoon area is not going to be as thick as the other spoons.

Now that you have finished your set of large spoons, check yourself by seeing if the curve on the end of the handle of all four spoons is the same. Your spoons should all be fairly close to the same thickness, with the exception of the egg spoon. The handle on all four spoons should be the same thickness and width. These four spoons will make a handsome decoration for your kitchen or dining area when hung on a rack of a different color wood than the spoons.

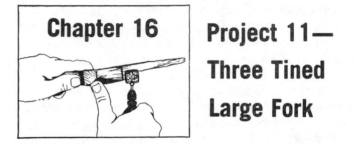

Chapter 16

Project 11— Three Tined Large Fork

Your next project is a three-tined large fork to go with your spoon set. Figure 16-1 is the photograph of the finished fork. Figure 16-2 is the scale drawing and silhouette view. The wood is 1-inch stock of whatever wood you were using for your spoons. Note that the handle is the same as it was on your spoons, including the curve on the end. The main difference in carving out the fork is that there is no hollowing-out process. However, it will take just a little extra care to get the curve of the fork (tines) just right. Check your silhouette view before starting so as to get this curve fixed firmly in mind. Note that the ends of the tines are just about in the center of your 1-inch piece of material.

CUTTING OUT THE TINES

Be careful in making your pattern, copying it onto your piece of wood and especially in cutting it out. If you cut out the tines as straight as possible, it will save a lot of time in working them down later. As with the spoons, start your carving from the front (point of the tines) to the back where it curves up into the handle. All this will be done with your coarse drum sander. To give yourself help in knowing where to bring the curve of the tines out at the end of the fork, draw two lines across the width of the end of the tines. These lines should be drawn apart the amount of thickness you want to wind up with on the end.

Fig. 16-1. Finished three-tined large fork.

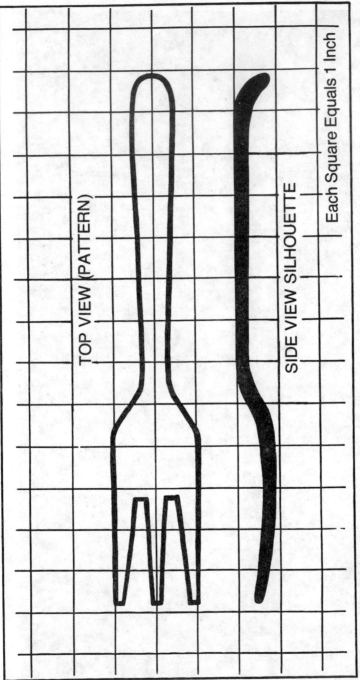

TOP VIEW (PATTERN)

SIDE VIEW SILHOUETTE

Each Square Equals 1 Inch

Fig. 16-2. Scale drawing and silhouette view of three-tined large fork.

138

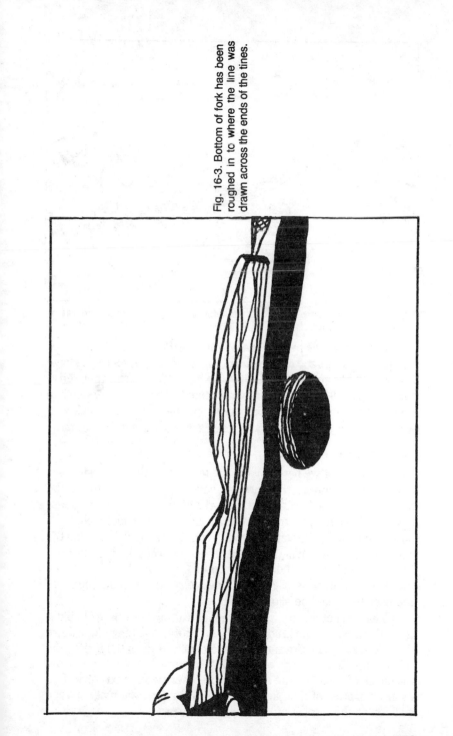

Fig. 16-3. Bottom of fork has been roughed in to where the line was drawn across the ends of the tines.

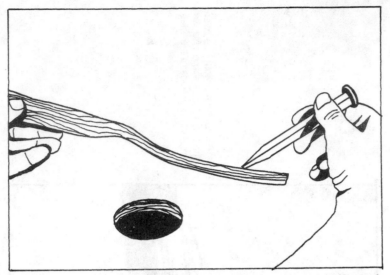

Fig. 16-4. Top of fork has been roughed in following the curve and thickness of the tines on the bottom.

In Fig. 16-3 we have cut away the wood where the fork curves up into the handle and on the end of the tines, up to where you have drawn your line across the width of the tines. The pencil is pointed at the line you will want to cut down to from the top of the fork. When you have reached this approximate shape, use a sanding block with #50 sandpaper to make sure your tines are all level with each other.

THE FINISHING PROCESS

In Fig. 16-4 we have turned the fork over and worked it down from the top, following the curve we have made on the bottom of the fork. Note that the thickness of the fork should be the same throughout the whole area, up to where it curves into the handle. Now cut down your handle the same as you did on your spoons, including the curve on the end. When this has been accomplished, start your finishing process by hand. As you do this, narrow down the tips of the tines just ever so slightly. The edge of the fork and the tines themselves should be slightly rounded.

There is nothing complicated about carving out your fork, but it is another good lesson in control of your Moto-tool. In working down the tine area, you will want to work from one side of the fork to the other, cutting away just one small layer after another. Keep the thickness of each tine the same as the other two as you work. It is mainly a matter of time and patience. Your fork will make a good addition to the display of your set of spoons.

Chapter 17

Project 12— Set of Small Spoons and Fork

This chapter is being included to give you a choice of size and handle design in a set of spoons and fork. Also, in actual usage the smaller spoons are a little easier to handle. The only difference in design is that there is no curve on the end of the handle. In this project, you will essentially be doing the same work as you did in Projects 10 and 11.

As the spoons and fork are almost identical to your large set, there is no need to include a photograph of the finished projects. Figure 17-1 is your scale drawing and silhouette view for the stirring spoon. Figure 17-2 is the drawing to show your hole pattern, Fig. 17-3 is your slotted spoon, Fig. 17-4 is your egg spoon and Fig. 17-5 is the scale drawing and silhouette view for your fork.

When working down the handles on your small spoon and fork set, the bottom of the handles should be left slightly rounded as opposed to the flat top. Try to make the spoon a little thinner than you have on the large set. Do the same with the fork. After you are working on them for a while, you will see this is necessary to make them look in proportion to the length and width as compared to your large set. Finish them up the same as the large set. If you want to display them on a rack with the large set, you might want to carve them out of a different color wood to provide an interesting contrast.

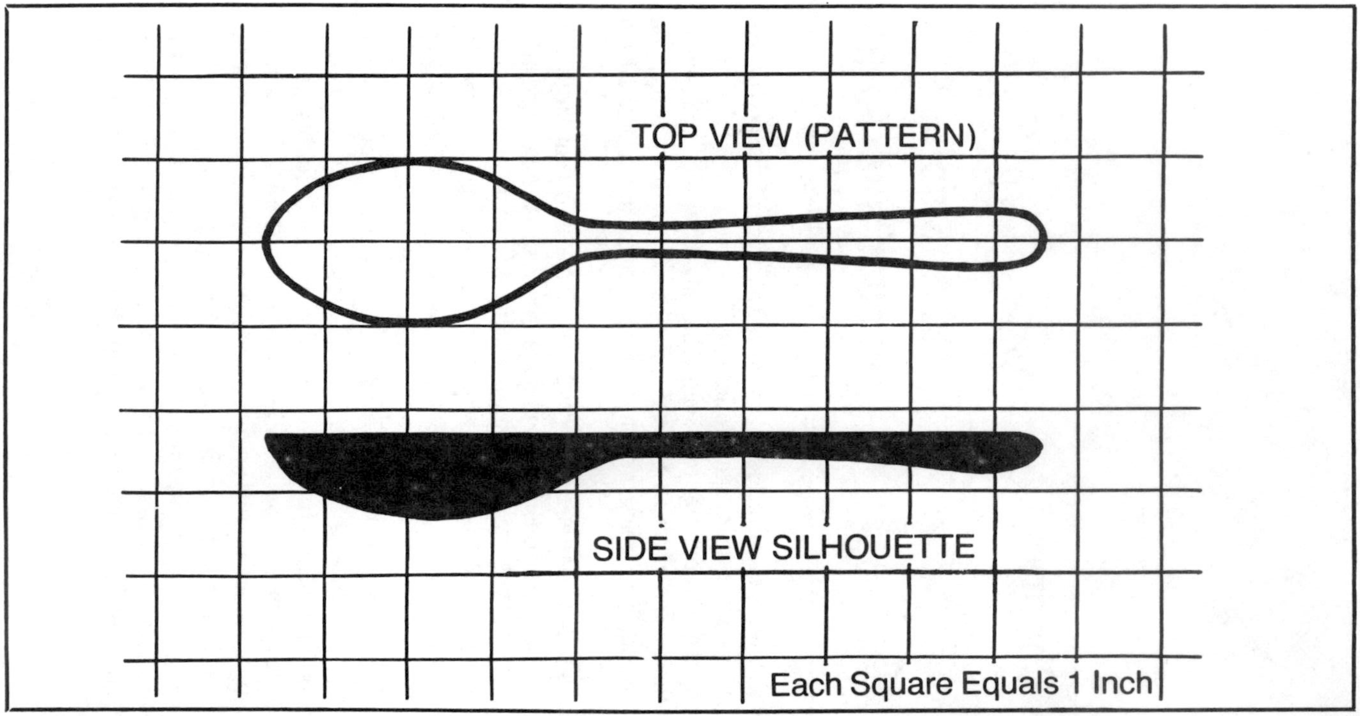

TOP VIEW (PATTERN)

SIDE VIEW SILHOUETTE

Each Square Equals 1 Inch

Fig. 17-1. Scale drawing and silhouette view for small mixing spoon.

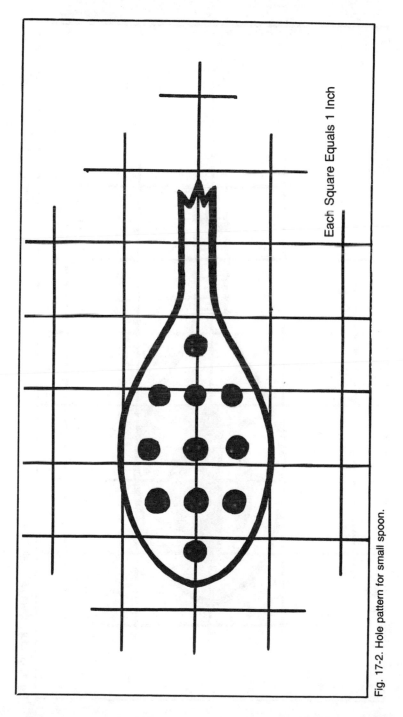

Each Square Equals 1 Inch

Fig. 17-2. Hole pattern for small spoon.

143

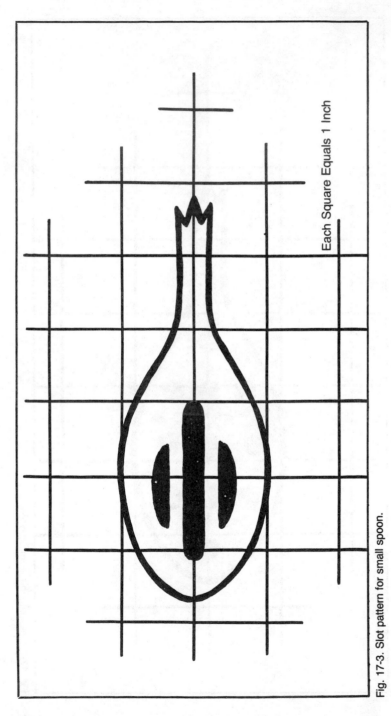

Each Square Equals 1 Inch

Fig. 17-3. Slot pattern for small spoon.

144

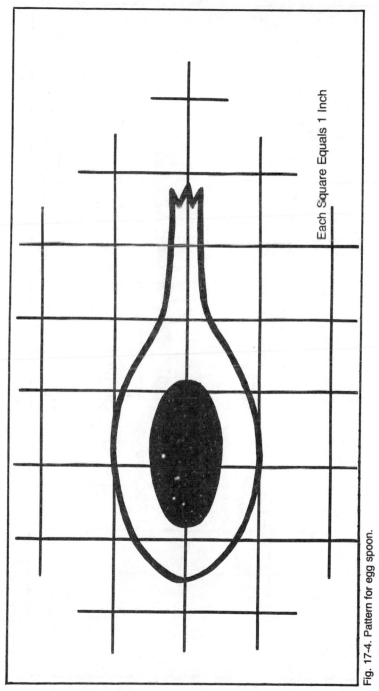

Each Square Equals 1 Inch

Fig. 17-4. Pattern for egg spoon.

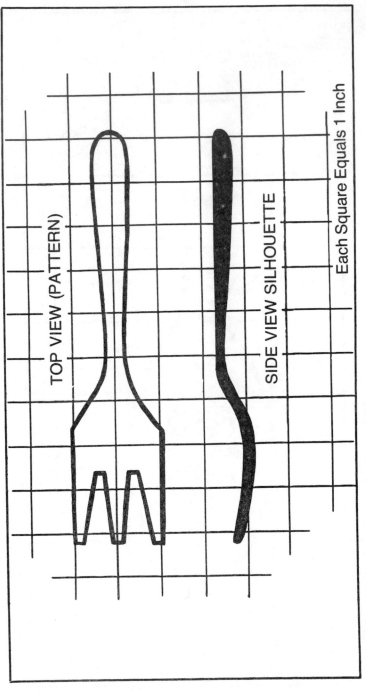

TOP VIEW (PATTERN)

SIDE VIEW SILHOUETTE

Each Square Equals 1 Inch

Fig. 17-5. Scale drawing and silhouette view for small fork.

Project 13— Relish Spoon

Chapter 18

This project goes a step further in teaching patience and control of your Moto-tool. Basically, you are making just another spoon the same length as your set of small spoons, and a curve on the end of the handle the same as the large set. It is, however, going to be thinner and narrower and require a more delicate touch than the others. Figure 18-1 is your finished project and Fig. 18-2 is your scale drawing and silhouette view.

CUTTING AND DRILLING

Start out the same as any other project. Draw your pattern, copy it off and cut out of 1-inch stock of whatever kind of wood you

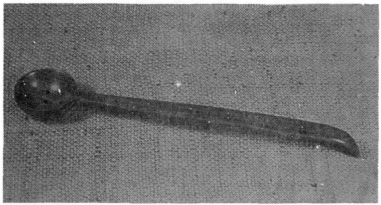

Fig 18-1. Finished relish spoon.

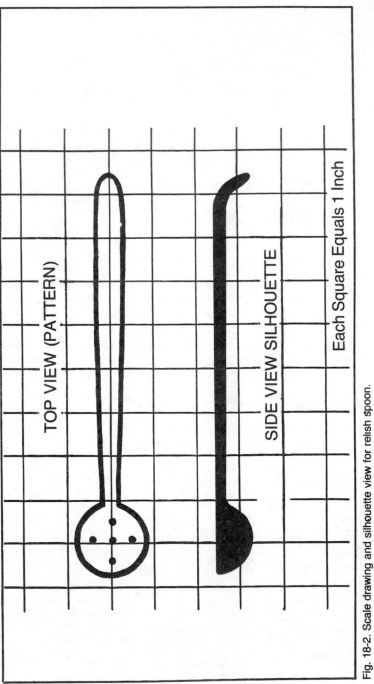

TOP VIEW (PATTERN)

SIDE VIEW SILHOUETTE

Each Square Equals 1 Inch

Fig. 18-2. Scale drawing and silhouette view for relish spoon.

want to use. The holes should be drilled from the bottom of the spoon, using a 7/64-inch drill bit. Start your carving from the bottom of the spoon and work it down to where it curves up into the handle. This spoon is different from the others in that the bowl part is a circle. To make your spoon look right, you must make sure it stays a circle. When you complete cutting down the bottom, it should look as if you had sliced a golf ball in half. Again, to help you accomplish this, draw an "X" mark in the center of the bottom of the bowl before you start your carving. Work towards the center of this "X" mark equally from all sides. Work the bottom of your relish spoon down to an almost finished condition before you start the hollowing-out process.

Before you start, draw in your line around the inside of the edge as you did your other spoons. In this case, you will want to make this line fairly close to the edge. Use your oval-steel cutter as you did for your other spoons, working around from one side to the other and from front to back. Keep your cutter going in a circle at all times. When you are about ready to smooth the bowl part down to see how thin you are getting it, wrinkle up a small square of #50 grade sandpaper. Place it in the bowl of the spoon and work it around and around with your thumb. Refer back to Fig. 18-1 and you will notice the edge is pretty thin. You will want to maintain this same thickness throughout the bowl, maybe just a trifle thicker on the bottom. Be very careful in working up to the edges with your drum sander, doing the last part by hand. It wouldn't take very much at this point to ruin your spoon by running your Moto-tool over the edge.

FINISHING THE JOB

Now work down the handle, leaving it almost flat on both top and bottom sides. When it is roughed in with your drum sander, use your sanding block again to keep your lines running straight. Do not attempt to enlarge the holes through the spoon. These holes are there to drain off any liquid from the relish without allowing any of the relish to escape. Finish your project by working down to your #600 wet or dry paper, wax and polish.

Your relish spoon makes a good addition to your collection of wooden kitchen utensils as well as being useful. It is very good for getting relish out of a jar and it looks very nice on the table with a relish dish.

Chapter 19

Pause for Reflection

Let's stop for just a moment to reflect on what we have been doing up to this point. You should by now be an expert in handling your Moto-tool. You can see why I said you can do anything with it that you can do with a knife or chisel and more. The sanding drum is used to rough in your carving. A stone cutter can be used to undercut. A sanding disc can be used to smooth down many hard to get to areas on your carving. The different steel cutters can be used to make a groove, to hollow something out, to make holes and even to rough in an object under certain circumstances. Your knives and chisels are used in combination with your Moto-tool when there is an area which needs to be cut down and you can't reach it any other way.

If you have completed all the projects up to this point, you should be developing a "feel" for the wood you are working with. You should be able to feel the amount of wood you are cutting away as you work with your drum sander or cutter. The more you practice carving out the type projects we have been making, the better "touch" you will develop. You will be better able to see the finished carving in your mind before you actually start.

If you didn't make your seahorse letter opener back at the start of the book, now is a good time to stop and go back to this project. If you tried it and had trouble with it before, you will find it will go along much easier now that you have made some of the easier projects.

ENJOY YOUR WORK

Ask yourself if you are satisfied with your finished carvings. Many times the tendency is to hurry through the project to obtain the finished carving without really enjoying the process of making it. Each step of the way, from start to finish, should be enjoyed as much as looking at the object you finally wind up with. If you are having trouble with one of your projects or you get tired of working on it and it becomes a chore instead of a joy, lay it aside and come back to it later. Work on something else for a change of pace.

Strive to improve your technique in carving with each project you work on. Do your tools feel awkward in your hands? With each carving you do, they should become more and more just an unconscious extension of your mind. This state comes with time and practice and only comes when the individual really enjoys his wood carving. You get to the point where you really don't have to think about the way you are holding your tools, but unconsciously know how they should be handled to get the effect you desire.

TAKE YOUR TIME

Don't try to hurry from being a beginner to becoming an expert in wood carving. Many times the individual wants to start off with too difficult a project. Then he gets discouraged when it turns out to be beyond his capabilities. Only when your simplest project turns out to be excellent is it time to proceed on to a more difficult carving. I didn't say perfect—only excellent. A wood carving can never be perfect except to someone who is satisfied with less than perfection. No matter how good you make your carving, you are always able to think of something you could have done to make it better. This is as it should be. It means your mind is working on something besides just making a copy.

The projects which follow will require you to use the same techniques and knowledge you have gained up to this point, but with a greater degree of expertise. Work through each one slowly and carefully so as to take another step forward in improving your carving skills. These projects were designed as exercises, to make you work just a little harder, while still adding to the collection of carvings you have already started. You will have made some carvings you can be proud of while still learning. A beginning piano student doesn't learn to play the piano by sitting down and immediately playing Bach. He starts out with a number of exercises to perform over and over again. These exercises will help him gain strength in his fingers and help him know where each note is on the keyboard without his having to think about it.

The same technique can be utilized by the wood carving student. The easier projects you work on, the stronger your hands will become and the less you will have to think about the actual mechanics of carving. Your mind tells you your carving should have a certain curve or angle to it and your hands automatically perform the mechanical part. You do have an important advantage over the piano student. While he cannot stop in the middle of a song and have it sound right, you can stop at any stage of your carving to see how it is progressing.

Project 14—
Set of
Three Spatulas

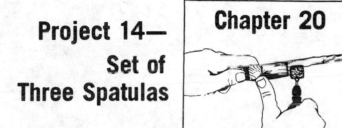

Chapter 20

This project is a set of three wooden spatulas for use with tefloncoated pans. One is solid, one has holes and the third has slots, just like your spoons. See Fig. 20-1 for your finished spatulas. Figure 20-2 is the scale drawing and silhouette. Figure 20-3 is a pattern for the spatula with holes and Fig. 20-4 is a pattern for the slots. In essence, you are making a fork without any tines which will be flat on the bottom. The handle will be the same as the handle on your small set of spoons. Your material is once again 1-inch walnut stock.

Now that you are getting a little more involved in your wood carving, you might want to pay more attention to your wood than just the kind used. To enhance the beauty of my collection, I have picked three different kinds of walnut. The solid spatula is carved from dark walnut. The spatula with holes is carved from a softer piece of walnut which has a very light grain running through it. The slotted spatula is made from a section of walnut which gives it the zebra-striped look.

WORKING DOWN THE SPATULA

I am not including any photographs of the actual carving as it is pretty much the same basic shape as your fork, without the curve of the tines. Make your pattern and cut out from whatever kind of wood you choose. Start your carving by cutting out the wood to make your curve from the bottom of the spatula into the handle. Check your silhouette view. Your spatula should be perfectly smooth on the bottom, so the next step is to use your sanding block and work down the bottom to take out all the little holes and grooves left by the

153

Fig. 20-1. Finished set of spatulas.

milling process. Use whatever grade of sandpaper you need to smooth it down, depending on how rough your piece of wood was on the bottom. Work it down almost to a finished stage.

When this has been accomplished, refer back to your silhouette view. Notice that there is a very slight upward sweep to the tip of the spatula and that it comes out to as sharp ann edge as you can make. This is to allow you to get the edge of the spatula under a fried egg or whatever is in your pan. Use your sanding drum across the width of your spatula to make this upward sweep on the end. Then go back to your sanding block to finish it in.

The next step is to turn the spatula over and start working it down from the top. This process should be started at the point where the handle curves down into the flat part of the spatula. Follow the line of curve you have made on the bottom. Work from there on out to the tip's edge, taking down one layer of wood at a time with your drum sander. As you work out towards the tip, you must work from side to side to keep your carving as flat as possible. This may

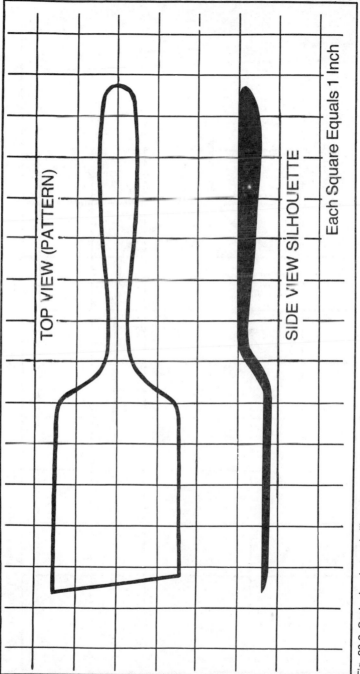

TOP VIEW (PATTERN)

SIDE VIEW SILHOUETTE

Each Square Equals 1 Inch

Fig. 20-2. Scale drawing and silhouette view for spatula.

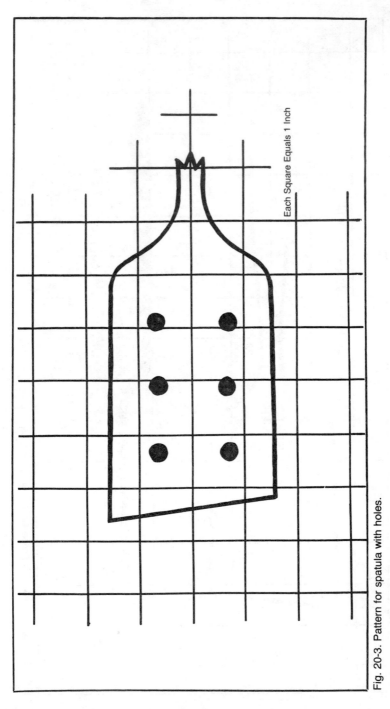

Each Square Equals 1 Inch

Fig. 20-3. Pattern for spatula with holes.

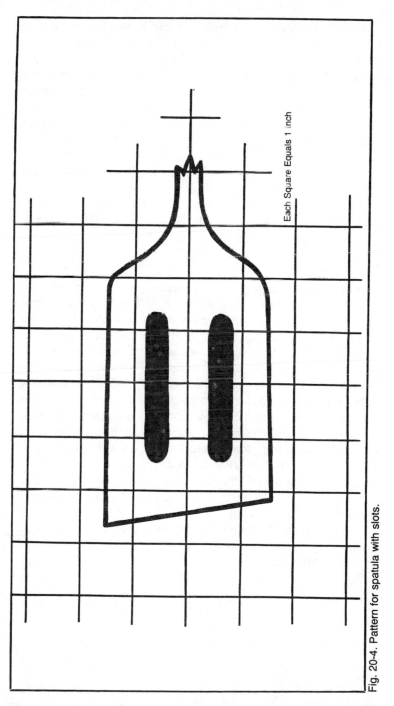

Each Square Equals 1 inch

Fig. 20-4. Pattern for spatula with slots.

sound easy, but after you actually get into it, you can see it is an excellent exercise in control. If you don't keep the top side of your spatula flat as you work it down, you can spend hours with a sanding block trying to reach the desired shape. This area must be as thin as possible without being so thin it will break in actual use. Use the thumb and forefinger technique to test your thickness as you work it down. Stop frequently to sight across the width of the spatula, making sure you are keeping this area level all the way down.

Now work down the handle the same as you did on your small set of spoons. The top of the handle should be flat. Curve the edges slightly and leave the bottom slightly rounded. This is mainly a matter of preference, except that in actual use this handle shape fits your hand better. The edges of the spatula should be slightly rounded with the exception of the tip.

SAND CAREFULLY

Pay particular attention to your finish sanding on this project. You will find a small blemish really stands out on a flat surface, whereas you might have gotten away with it on a curved or angled surface. Use your sanding block on the flat surface of the spatula and work out to the tip. Since you have already sanded the bottom down almost to a finished stage, you will work mainly on the top side at this time. As you continue to sand it down to gain the desired thickness, keep checking to see if you are getting close to the slightly curved-up tip which you have cut in from the bottom. If you reach the thickness you want and still haven't come to a sharp edge at the tip, work a little more curve into it from the bottom to finish up with. Your spatula should not be more than 1/8-inch thick.

Upon completion of this project, you can see why I am so enthused about the Moto-tool for wood carving. Can you imagine carving this out with a knife?

Now make the other two spatulas, making your holes and slots the same way you did on your spoons. Remember to drill your holes from the bottom side.

Project 15—
Scoop

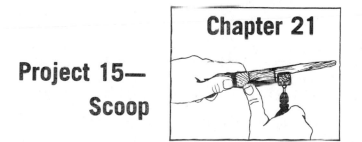

Chapter 21

This project is another step forward in your exercises to improve your technique and control. You will be working on a larger project. It will include flat surfaces as well as a much larger curved area to contend with. You will find that the larger the curved surface you are working on, the harder it is to keep it symmetrical. For this project, you will need a block of walnut (or other wood) 2-1/2 inches square and 10 inches long. Figure 21-1 is a photograph of your finished scoop and Fig. 21-2 is your scale drawing and silhouette view. On this project you will want to make a pattern of the side or silhouette view. To cut out your scoop, you will need a saber saw. It would be easier to cut out on a band saw if one is available. After you have made your pattern of the side view, copy it off on your block of wood. If one side of your piece of wood is rougher than the others, that side should be used for the top as it will all be cut away.

USING THE SABER SAW

First, cut out the area where the bottom of the scoop curves up into the handle and along the length of the handle on out to the end. You should cut well on the outside of your line in case you don't hold your saw perfectly straight. Don't cut the curve on the open end of the scoop at this time. Lay your block down on your workbench with the top of the scoop down and draw in your handle from the end to where it meets the scoop. The areas on each side of the handle should be cut out with your saber saw. In effect, you are just cutting a handle out of your block of wood. By drawing your line on, and cutting from, the bottom of the scoop, you still have the flat surface of the top to lay on your workbench to hold it steady while you cut with your saber saw. Again, because it is difficult to hold your saber saw straight and because it will cut fairly rough, cut well to the outside of your lines to give yourself plenty of wood to work with. Refer now to Fig. 21-3. This photograph gives you a pretty good idea of what you wind up with after you have cut the handle out with your saber saw.

We are now starting to cut down the edges of the scoop to make the curve on the bottom (Fig. 21-3). You will notice I have drawn a line down the center of my block of wood to give me help in keeping it symmetrical. I have done this on both the top and bottom. Don't try to take it down very far. This is one project you must continually work one spot to another to keep the shape you want.

ROUNDING OFF AND ROUGHING IN THE HANDLE

Now move on to Fig. 21-4. Here, we are cutting away the excess wood from the bottom of the handle and rounding it off. Notice how little I have taken down the edges of the scoop on the bottom before I moved on to the handle. At this point, I have also been working in the curve from the scoop to the handle. Keep referring to your silhouette view as you work.

When the bottom of your handle has been roughed in the desired shape, turn the scoop over and start roughing in the top of the handle. In Fig. 21-5 we have cut the handle down slightly from the top level of the scoop with our drum sander and are starting to work on out to the end. Make sure to keep a curve in the top back of the scoop when you cut in the handle. This curve will be maintained as nearly as possible down the back side and on the bottom of the scoop. This is one reason for not cutting down the edges of the bottom of the scoop too far before establishing this curve on the top. Go ahead and completely rough in your handle at this time.

Now go on to Fig. 21-6. The handle has been roughed in and we are going back to the bottom and the back side of the scoop since we have our curve established on the top. Remember that the sides of the scoop are going to remain flat about two-thirds of the way down from the top. As you work from one side to the other to make the curve on the bottom, stop and sight down the length of the scoop to

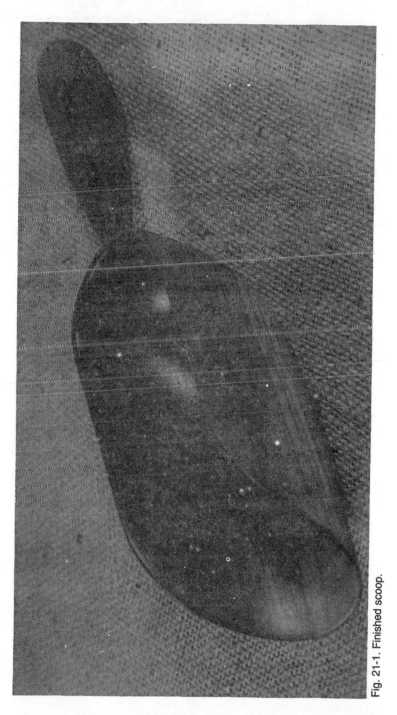

Fig. 21-1. Finished scoop.

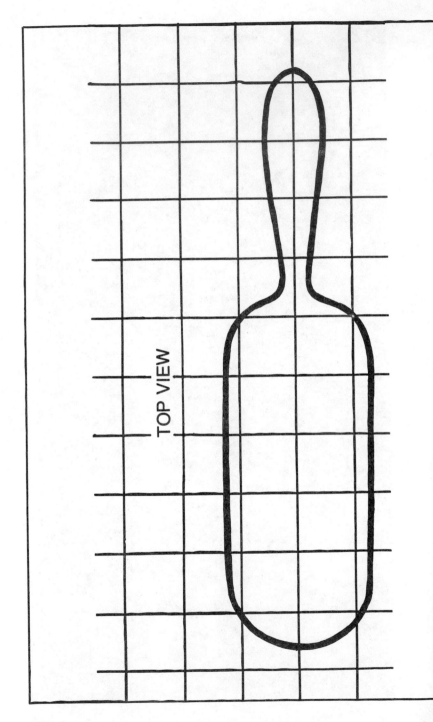

TOP VIEW

162

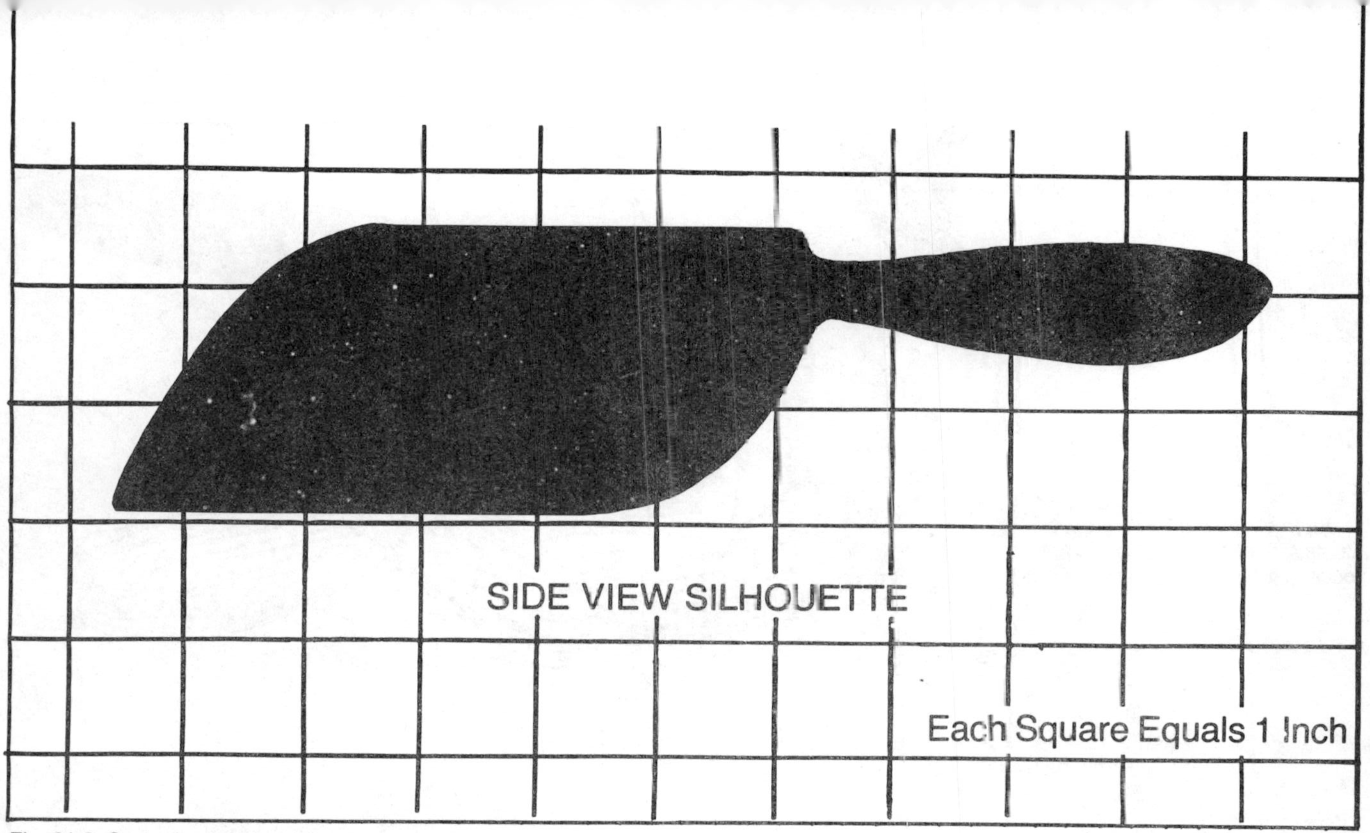

SIDE VIEW SILHOUETTE

Each Square Equals 1 Inch

Fig. 21-2. Scale drawing and silhouette view for scoop.

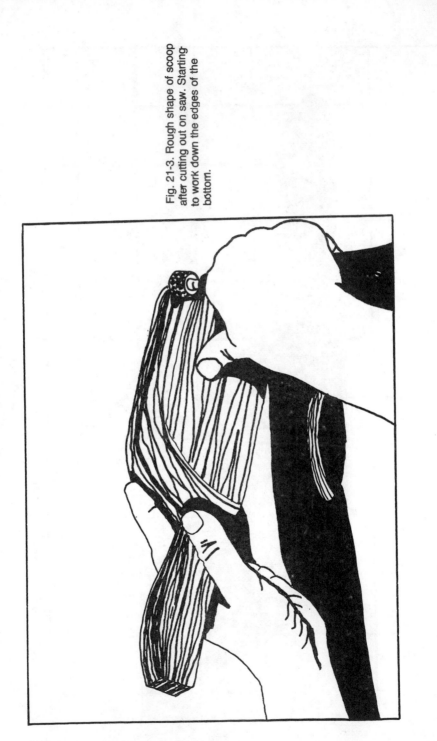

Fig. 21-3. Rough shape of scoop after cutting out on saw. Starting to work down the edges of the bottom.

make sure you are cutting down both sides equally and are maintaining the curve from the top. Stop before you have it completely roughed in. Use your sanding block to work down the flat part of the sides, keeping them parallel to each other.

WORKING IN THE CURVE

Now we go to the front or open end of the scoop which we have been ignoring up to this point. In Fig. 21-7, we are drawing in a

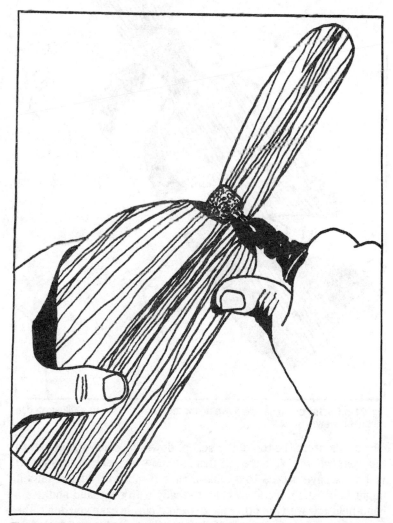

Fig. 21-4. Rough in and cut away excess wood from bottom of handle.

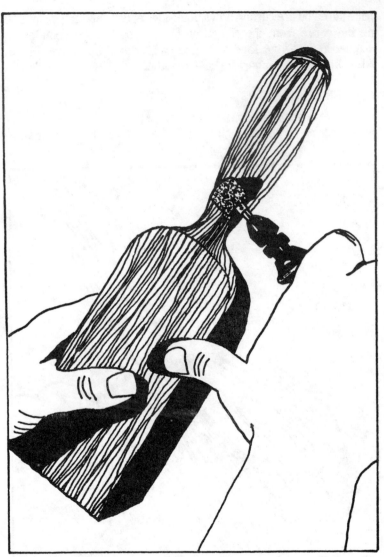

Fig. 21-5. Cut top of the handle down below the top of the scoop as illustrated in silhouette view.

curved line from the top of the scoop, down the sides and on out to the *front bottom*. We have left this until now for several reasons. If you don't have access to a table-mounted saber or a band saw, it might be a little difficult to hold it steady with one hand and use a hand-held saw with the other hand to cut it out. In case you don't, the following procedure is to be followed. First, make your pen line

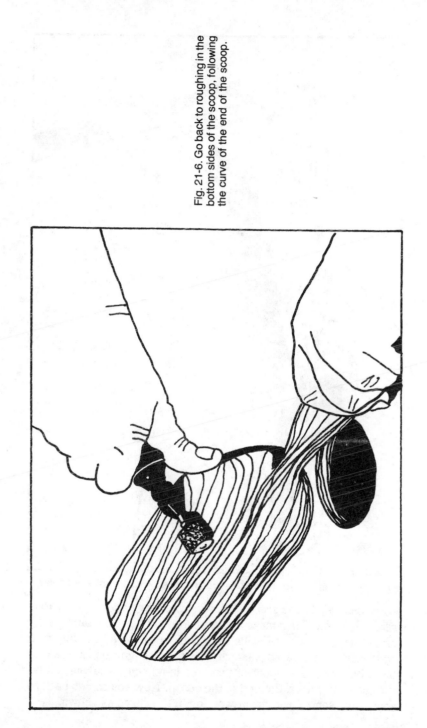

Fig. 21-6. Go back to roughing in the bottom sides of the scoop, following the curve of the end of the scoop.

Fig. 21-7. Draw in curve on the end of the scoop as shown on the silhouette view.

down one side of the scoop, following the curve as shown on your silhouette view. Then make a paper pattern of this curve and copy it off on the other side to make sure both sides are even. Now take whatever saw is available and cut straight through from one side to the other, removing most of this area in one cut. You will just be cutting a triangle off the end of the scoop. Now you can go back to your drum sander and finish working in the curve as shown.

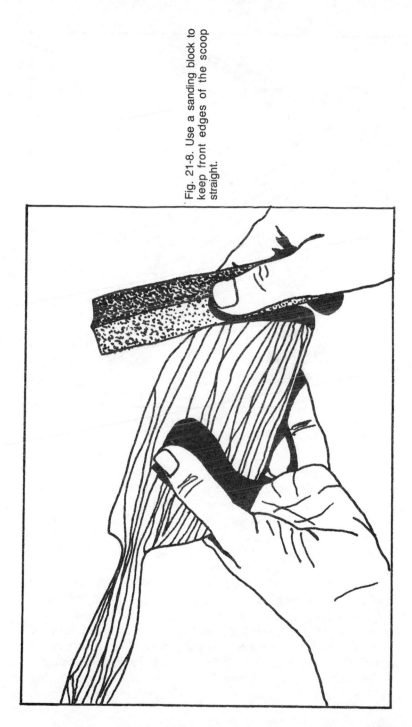

Fig. 21-8. Use a sanding block to keep front edges of the scoop straight.

169

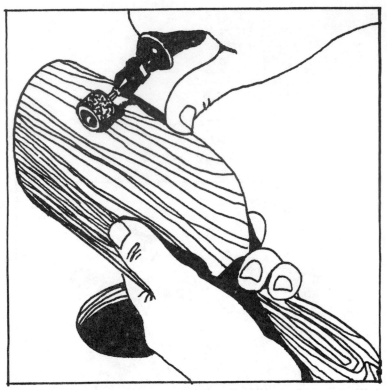

Fig. 21-1-9. Now finish working in the curve across the bottom of the scoop. Work it down to an almost finished stage at this stage.

To keep both sides even, we then go back to our sanding block to finish taking this area down (Fig. 21-8). As you work with your sanding block, make sure you keep it straight and stop frequently to sight across the front. It is very important to get both sides even in length at this time. If you don't, it might not show up very much now. When you get the scoop hollowed out, though, it will really show up and you will have a lopsided scoop.

Going on to Fig. 21-9, we have the curve on the front of the scoop and have gone back to our sanding drum to finish working in the curve across the bottom and the back. As you work down the curve across the back, you will need to work on the area where the handle makes a sharp curve into the scoop. Make sure you are working the wood down equally from front to back. When you are satisfied with the general shape you have, go back to your sanding block and start working it down along the length and from one side to the other. Work it down to an almost finished stage before stopping this step of the process.

HOLLOWING OUT THE INSIDE

We now have the outside of the scoop worked down to semi-finished stage. All that remains is to hollow out the inside.

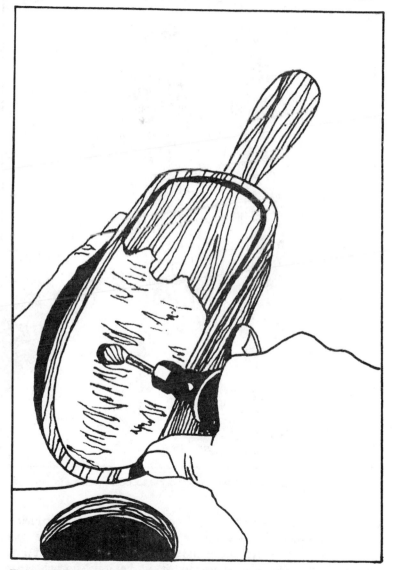

Fig. 21-10. Start hollowing out the scoop from the front with an oval steel cutter. Work from one side to the cther.

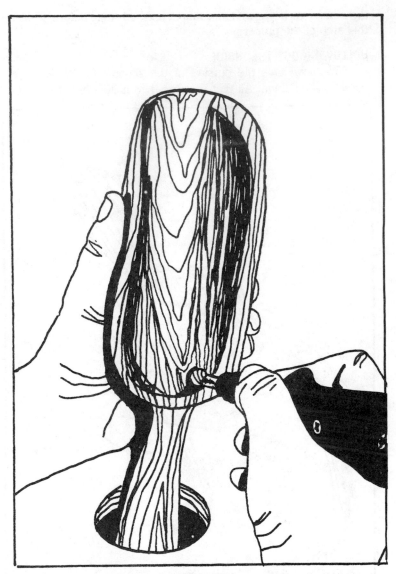

Fig. 21-11. Make sure the back bottom part of the scoop is the same thickness as the sides.

Using your pen, draw a line around the area which you want to hollow out, slightly wider than you will want it when finished. Change your Moto-tool to a steel oval cutter and start cutting from the front (Fig. 21-10). This is a fairly large area to cut out, but it will go faster than you think if you don't try to go too fast!

Use the same technique you learned from hollowing out your spoons. Use a pencil grip on your Moto-tool and cut away one layer of wood after another, working from the front and from one side to the other. As you continue to cut in from the top front, keep cutting in further towards the back. Use your thumb and forefinger technique to keep it equally thick on the sides and bottom.

In Fig. 21-11 we have worked all the way to the back. The tendency here is to leave too much thickness in this area, especially at the bottom. Take your time in this area. Notice that the scoop is quite a bit thicker here than in the photograph of the finished project. When we have hand-sanded it down to get all those grooves and ridges left by the cutter, it will be just about right.

Now change back to your drum sander and smooth down the sides as shown in Fig. 21-12. By inserting your Moto-tool in from the front, you can use it to smooth down the bottom. The back bottom area is the only part which will have to be completely worked down by hand.

Fig. 21-12. Use your sanding drum to help in smoothing down the inside of the sides and the bottom of the scoop.

You should now be ready for your finish sanding. As you do this, leave the edges of the scoop slightly rounded (not sharp). Again, pay particular attention to your finish sanding as it would take only a small blemish to ruin the appearance of your project. Finish by waxing and buffing to a gloss.

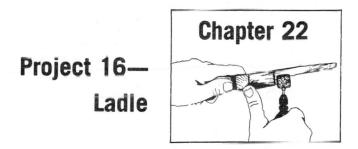

Project 16— Ladle

Chapter 22

Here is another project to improve your carving skills, while still adding to your collection of kitchen utensils. This ladle is just the right size to use in dipping hot soup from a kettle. Figure 22-1 is the photograph of your finished ladle and Fig. 22-2 is your scale drawing and silhouette view. Your material is a block of walnut (or other wood) 2-1/2 inches square and 9-1/2 inches long. Again, on this project you will need a saber saw or band saw to cut it out. Make your pattern of the top view and copy it off on your block of wood.

MAKING THE CUTS

Start cutting out the circle of the ladle first. From there, cut out *one* side of the handle. Now draw in a line with your pen from the bottom of the ladle up to where it meets the handle, and on out to the end of the handle. This line must be drawn on the side of the handle which has already been cut out. Because you have not yet cut out the other side of the handle, you have a flat surface to place against your workbench to help in holding it steady while cutting out this area. See Fig. 22-3. I left the handle quite thick when cutting this area out. Now lay your ladle down on your workbench on the top, which is also a flat surface, and draw in the other side of the handle on the bottom surface. Cut this out and you will wind up with the ladle as shown in Fig. 22-3. Following these steps will allow you a flat surface throughout your cutting.

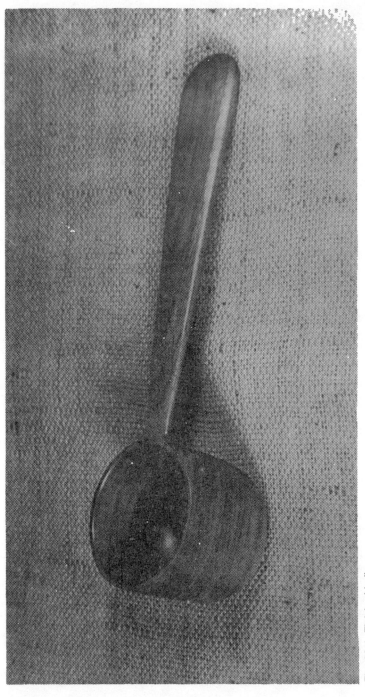

Fig. 22-1. Finished ladle.

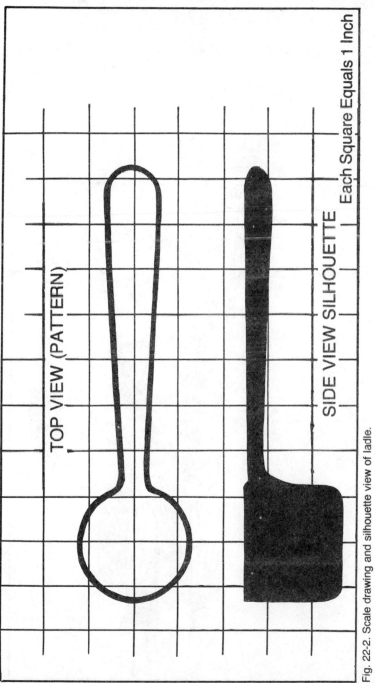

TOP VIEW (PATTERN)

SIDE VIEW SILHOUETTE

Each Square Equals 1 Inch

Fig. 22-2. Scale drawing and silhouette view of ladle.

177

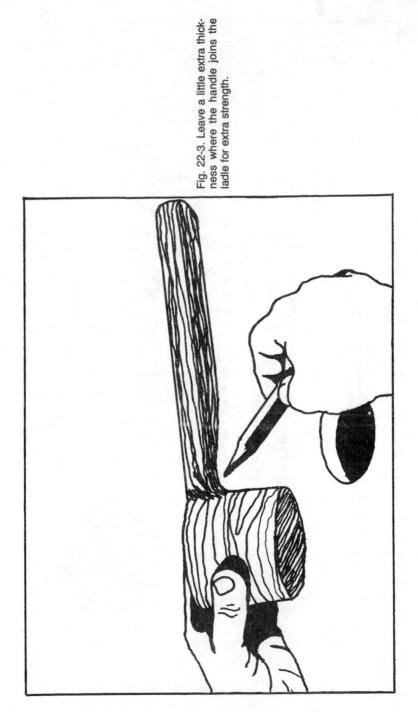

Fig. 22-3. Leave a little extra thickness where the handle joins the ladle for extra strength.

Notice the curve from the handle into the ladle. We want to leave this area fairly thick to give the handle strength. Take your time in cutting it out. The closer you cut to your lines, the less actual carving you will have to do.

We are again working with a circle. Draw in your pen line around the area you want to hollow out. This line should be drawn in

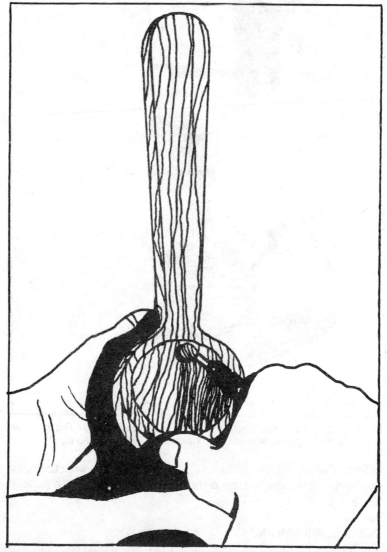

Fig. 22-4. Use an oval cutter to make the initial cut around the inside of the line you have drawn.

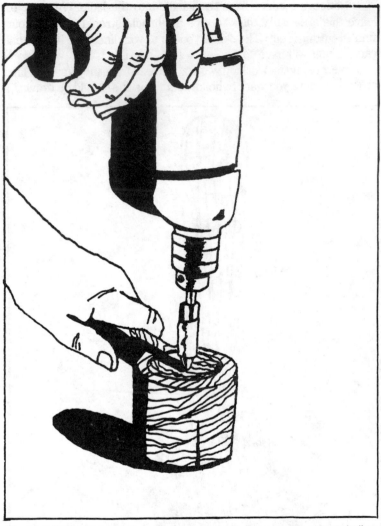

Fig. 22-5. Drill a 1/2-inch hole down the center of the area you are going to hollow out to the depth you have marked on your drill bit with masking tape.

to leave the sides almost twice as thick as you actually want them, as you have not yet worked down the outside of the ladle to a perfect circle.

DRILLING AND SANDING

The first step is to sand down the bottom of the ladle until it is perfectly smooth and level with the top. You will want to have an almost finished surface to work towards from the top. Now use your steel oval cutter to cut around on the inside of your line on the top as illustrated in Fig. 22-4. Don't cut out any more at this time.

The next step is to drill a 1/2-inch hole down through the center of your ladle from the top (Fig. 22-5). Hold your drill bit on the outside of your ladle and mark the depth you want to drill to by placing a piece of masking tape around the bit. You will want to drill down to where the point of the bit stops at a thickness of twice what you want it when finished.

Now go back to your drum sander and start working down the outside of the ladle. Keep as perfect a circle as possible on the ladle. Finish it off by hand so you will have a good surface to work toward when you start hollowing it out from the inside.

Change to your steel oval cutter and start cutting out the inside just as you have on your other projects. Work from the hole you have drilled to the outside and down, taking off just a layer at a time. When you get to the bottom of the hole you have drilled, stop and change back to your drum sander to work down the sides a little more smoothly and to the thickness you want. The inside bottom of the ladle must be worked down entirely by hand with a piece of # 50 sandpaper.

When the bowl on your ladle has been completed, move on to the handle and work it down with your drum sander. Check your silhouette view. Notice the top of the handle is cut down slightly which will leave a *rim* all the way around the bowl part. The handle on your ladle should be a little larger than the handles on your spoons when completed. Now go on to your procedure in finish sanding, waxing and buffing and your ladle is complete.

Chapter 23

Project 17—
Potato Masher

Our next project will be an old-fashioned potato masher. Figure 23-1 is our finished project and Fig. 23-2 is the scale drawing and end view. Our material is a block of walnut approximately 2-1/2 inches square and 10 inches long.

This project is very easy to make as long as you follow all the techniques you have learned thus far. If you get in too much of a rush, you are going to wind up with a potato masher that is either lopsided or will have a crooked handle. For this reason, stay fairly close to the steps as they are presented here. Again, you are going to need a band saw or a saber saw to cut your project out because of the thickness of the wood.

MAKING PATTERNS

Make your pattern from the scale drawing and copy it off on your block of wood. In Fig. 23-3 you will notice we have not tried to stay too close to your lines when cutting it out. You want to have plenty of wood to work with.

Now draw in your handle on the portion of the handle which has already been cut out. Just sketch this in rather loosely. When you cut it out, stay well to the outside of your line. Your piece of wood is going to be rather hard to hold steady because there is not much of a flat surface at this point. There is another reason for not trying to cut your handle in exactly to size right now, and we will go into that in just a few minutes. See Fig. 23-4.

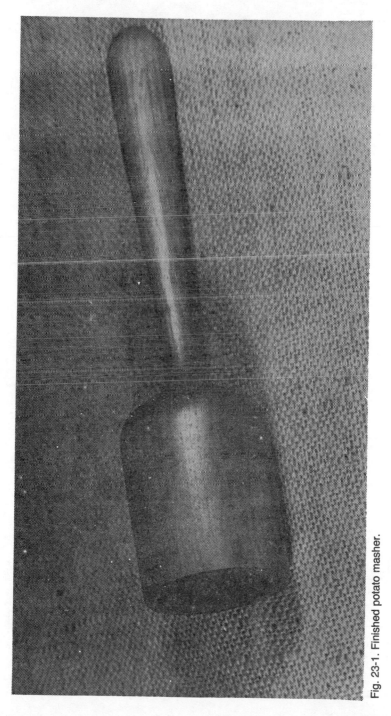

Fig. 23-1. Finished potato masher.

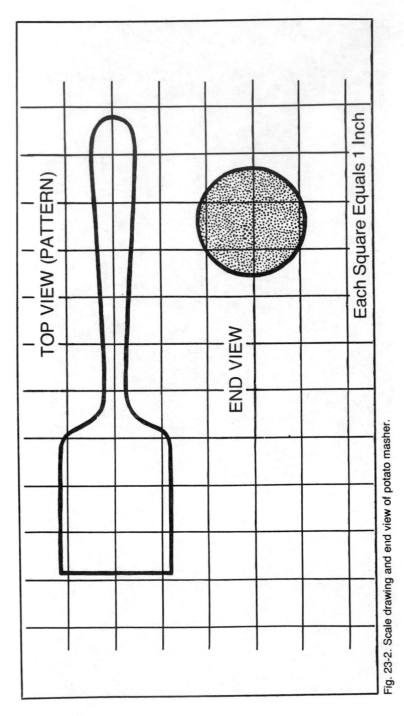

TOP VIEW (PATTERN)

END VIEW

Each Square Equals 1 Inch

Fig. 23-2. Scale drawing and end view of potato masher.

Now make a pattern of the end of the potato masher and draw it in on the end of your block. Draw this in as exact as you can get it. See Fig. 23-5. Using your drum sander, start working down the edges of your block of wood as shown in Fig. 23-6. After each edge has been worked off a little, start working around and around your masher to get it as perfect a circle as possible. Don't work com-

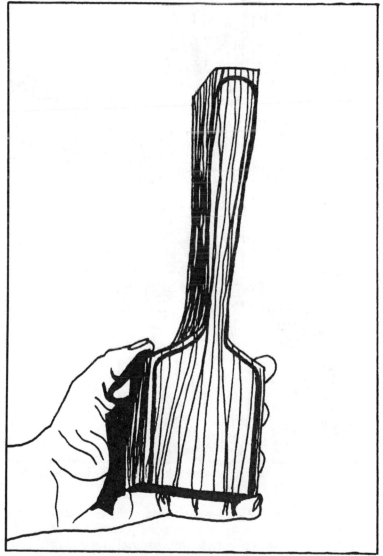

Fig. 23-3. First saw cut on potato masher.

Fig. 23-4. Sketch in handle on already cut-out portion of handle, then cut out. Don't cut too close to your line.

pletely down to the line you have drawn in on the end. Notice in Fig. 23-6 we are leaving a small margin of wood outside our line. The main thing right now is to get it all worked down to as good a circle as possible without going clear down to your pattern size.

WORKING DOWN THE HANDLE

When this has been accomplished, start taking off the edges of the handle and working it down to the size you want it. In Fig. 23-7 we are starting this process by working from the masher part out toward the end of the handle. As you work your way out toward the end of the handle, stop very frequently and sight down your potato

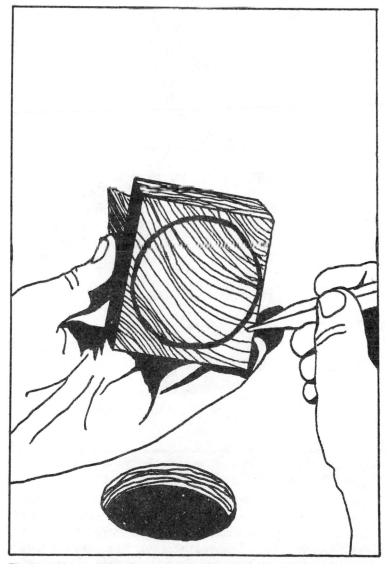

Fig. 23-5. Make pattern of end view and draw in or end of potato masher.

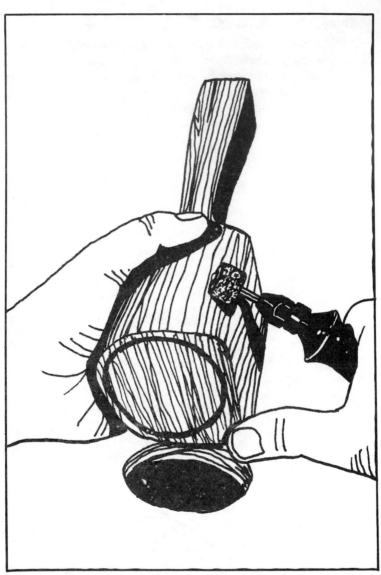

Fig. 23-6. Rounding off the edges of the masher with the drum sander. Do not work completely down to pattern line.

masher. As you sight down the length, slowly turn the masher part, which you have already made as perfect a circle as you can, and see if the handle remains in a straight line with the masher part or whether it wobbles as you turn it. This was the reason for leaving the handle quite a bit larger than pattern size when cutting it out. If the handle wobbles just a little while you are sighting down the length and turning it, it means that it is not running in a straight line from the masher. You still have enough wood left to take one side of the handle down more than the others and not wind up with too small a handle.

When you are satisfied you have your handle running in a straight line, work it on down to size. Use your sanding block as

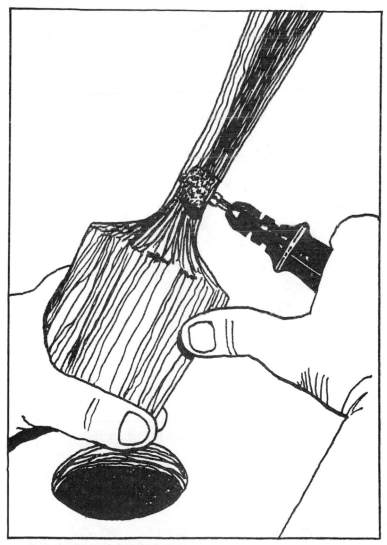

Fig. 23-7. Starting to rough in handle.

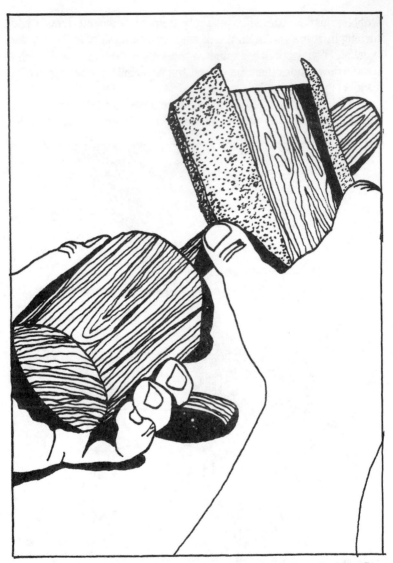

Fig. 23-8. Use a sanding block to maintain a straight line throughout handle.

shown in Fig. 23-8 to take out all the small bumps from your rough sanding with the sanding drum.

WORKING ON THE MASHER END

Now go back to the other (masher) end and finish cutting it down the line you have drawn in on the end. Do this by using your

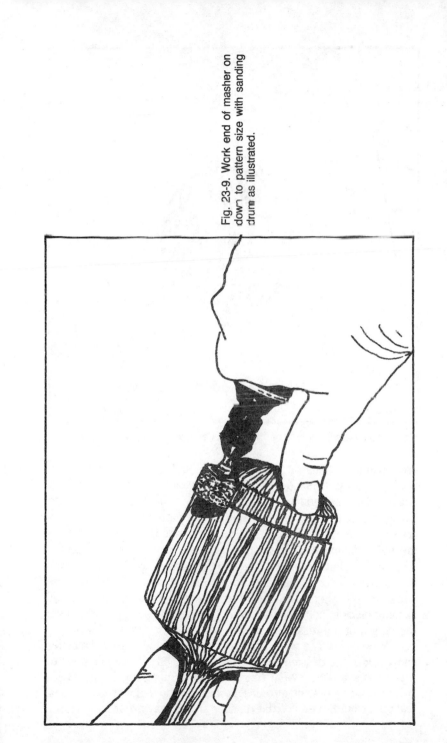

Fig. 23-9. Work end of masher on down to pattern size with sanding drum as illustrated.

Fig. 23-10. Use stiff paper pattern to check end of the masher for size.

drum sander as illustrated in Fig. 23-9. Just cut down an area the width of your drum sander. Make a pattern out of stiff paper and cut out the circle as shown in Fig. 23-10. When the end of your potato masher fits snugly through the hole in your pattern, stop cutting this area down. Notice in Fig. 23-10 the small arrow I have drawn in on the end of the masher. This was an area which was just a little larger than it should have been. I drew in the arrow so I wouldn't lose track of that spot before I had a chance to cut it down. Now continue working your way up the masher, using your sanding drum and sanding block in combination until you can slide your pattern down the length of the masher.

Now go back to where the handle curves out into the masher and work in the desired curve. See Fig. 23-11. You don't want to make too sharp a curve at this point. Continuing on to Fig. 23-12, work the curve out and into the masher part so that it stops an equal distance from the end of the masher all the way around the circle.

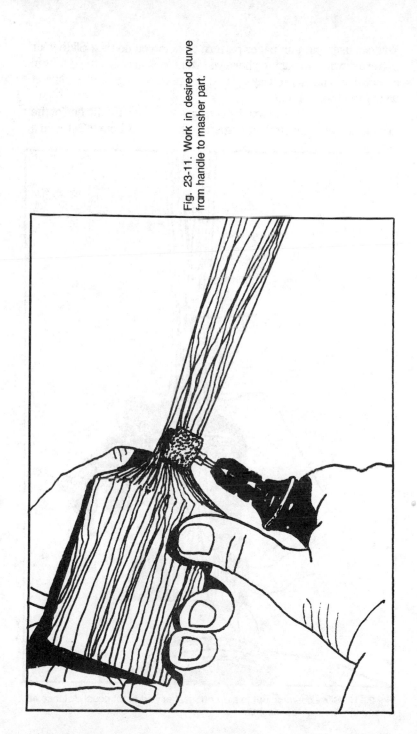

Fig. 23-11. Work in desired curve from handle to masher part.

You can use your stiff paper pattern to help you do this. Slide your pattern down to the point where you want the curve to stop. Draw in a very light line all the way around the masher to give you a line at which to stop.

The last step in the rough carving is to make sure the end of the masher is perfectly straight across. In Fig. 23-13 I have fastened a

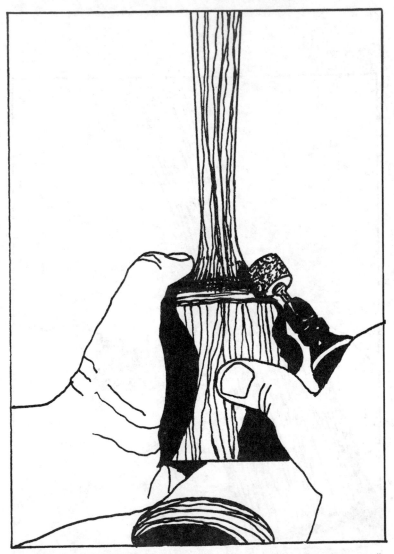

Fig. 23-12. Carry curve on out to stop on masher part at an equal distance all around the circle of the masher.

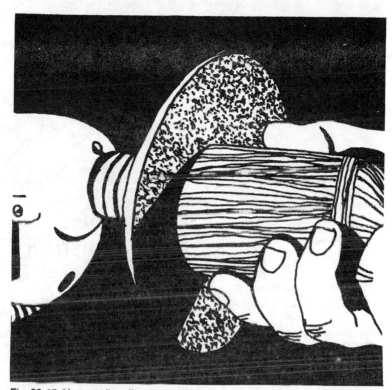

Fig. 23-13. Use sanding disc to straighten up and finish the end of the masher.

hand drill with a sanding disc in a vise and am sanding off the end to make it straight. Don't put your hand drill in a vise if it is made of plastic. All that is left to do now is the finish sanding, waxing and buffing.

Chapter 24

Project 18—
Meat Tenderizer

No set of kitchen utensils is complete without a meat tenderizer. This is a very simple project to make and you should be able to complete it in a very short amount of time. Figure 24-1 is your finished project. Figure 24-2 is your scale drawing and silhouette view. Figure 24-3 is the end view of the head of the tenderizer. For this project, your material will consist of a block of walnut 2 inches square and approximately 3-1/2 inches long for the head of the tenderizer. The handle will be made separately and can be cut from a standard 1-inch piece of walnut stock.

MAKING THE TENDERIZER PATTERNS

The handle should be carved first. Make your pattern and cut it out from your 1-inch piece of stock. When making your pattern, be sure to include the end which sticks up into the head of the tenderizer. You have made enough handles so that we won't go into any of the mechanics of the actual carving. Check your scale drawing, silhouette view and photograph of the finished meat tenderizer to get the shape of the handle well in mind before you start. Work it down to the finished stage before proceeding with the head of the tenderizer.

Make your pattern for the head of the tenderizer and cut it out from your block of walnut. It should be a perfect rectangular block of wood. Some meat tenderizers are this shape, but we are going to cut ours down as shown by the end view to give it a little better

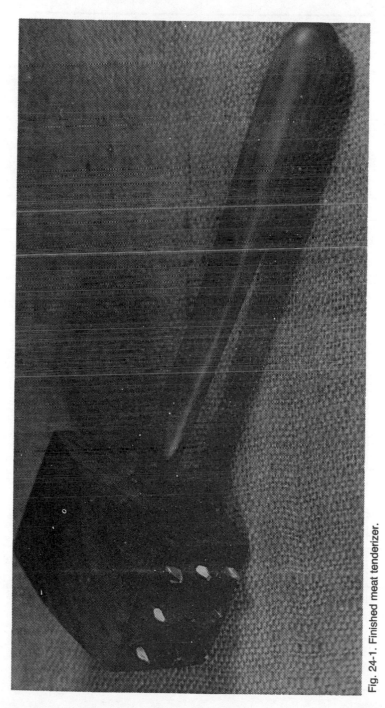

Fig. 24-1. Finished meat tenderizer.

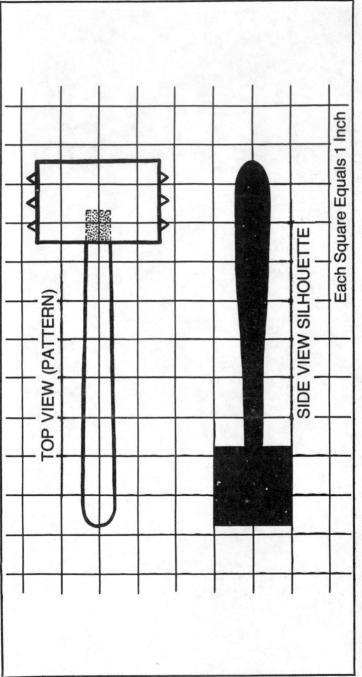

TOP VIEW (PATTERN)

SIDE VIEW SILHOUETTE

Each Square Equals 1 Inch

Fig. 24-2. Scale drawing and silhouette view of meat tenderizer.

appearance. Make a pattern for the end view and copy it off on your block of wood. In Fig. 24-4 we are using the drum sander to rough in the desired shape. Use your sanding block to make sure the surfaces you have cut down are level.

INSERTING THE HANDLE

The next step is to cut out a hole in the exact center of the block in which to insert the handle. In Fig. 24-5 we have drawn a line from one corner of the block to the other in an "X" pattern to locate the center. Hold the end of your handle in the center of the "X" and draw around it very lightly to indicate the area you want to cut out. Remember, you are going to want to cut out an area smaller than the area you have drawn in. Note in Fig. 24-5 we are using a small round steel cutter. Start from the center and keep working out toward the edge of the area you have drawn in. Keep trying the end of the handle in the hole you are cutting out to check for size. It should be a very snug fit. When you have the hole to the right shape, go ahead and cut it in to the depth you want. As you cut it in, keep checking to make sure you are cutting the hole in so that the handle will stick out at a right angle from the bottom of the tenderizer. When you have the correct fit, coat the end of the handle which fits into the tenderizer

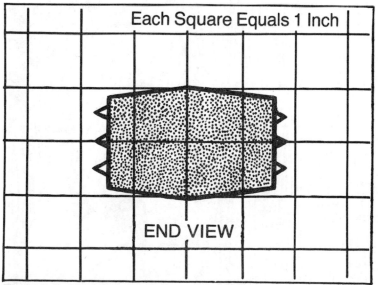

Fig. 24-3. End view of the head of a meat tenderizer.

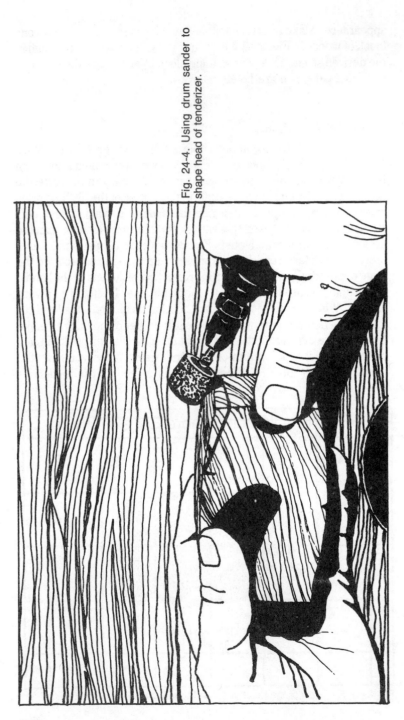

Fig. 24-4. Using drum sander to shape head of tenderizer.

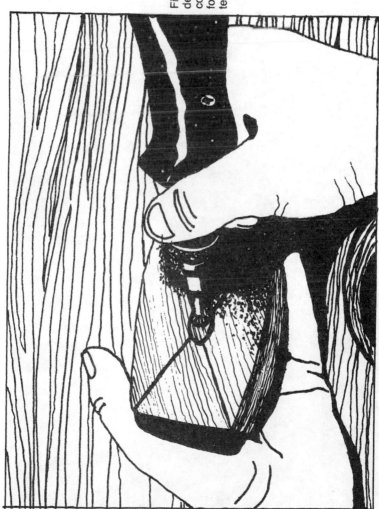

Fig. 24-5. Locate center of tenderizer by drawing an "x" from one corner to the other. Then cut out hole for the handle with small round cutter.

Fig. 24-6. Draw in pattern for nail holes and then center punch before drilling.

head with epoxy glue and fit it into place. Allow it to dry for at least 24 hours before proceeding any further.

NAILING

When your handle has thoroughly dried in place, proceed on to the next step. Most machine-made meat tenderizers have a series of

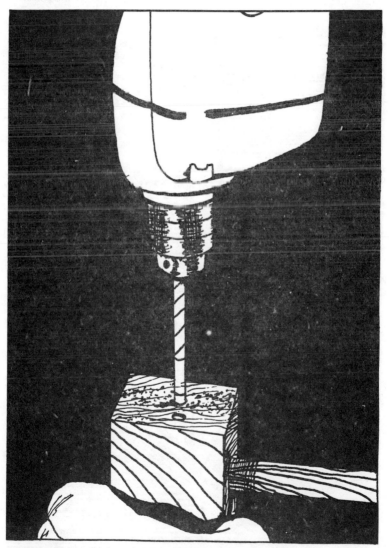

Fig. 24-7. Drill holes for nails to the desired depth marked by masking tape or the drill bit.

horizontal and vertical grooves cut into each end of the head which produces several rows of triangular points. We are going to install three rows of nails, three across, to create this effect. In actual use, it does a much better job of tenderizing your meat, anyway. You will need 18 #56 common aluminum nails. You want to use the aluminum nails so they will not rust. The point of the nail is most generally 1/4 inch in length. We want to sink 1/2 inch of the nail into the head of the

Fig. 24-8. Pounding nails in place with the point outwards.

tenderizer, so measure off all your nails 3/4 inch down from the point and cut them off with a hack saw. You will have just the point of the nail protruding out of the wood.

In Fig. 24-6 we have marked, with pen, the three rows, three across, where we want to drill the holes for the nails. I have not included a pattern for the holes as you might want to use a smaller nail and make rows of four. The choice is up to you. Just make sure they are evenly spaced across the head of the tenderizer. In Fig. 24-6 you will notice I am using a large needle to center punch my marks before drilling. I find a large needle is much more effective in use than a regular center punch as you can better see where you are placing the point.

Now choose a drill bit of a size which will allow the nail to be driven snugly into the hole. Try it on a scrap block of wood first. You will want the hole of a size such that the nail cannot be pushed into it by hand, but which will not be so snug you can't easily drive it in with a hammer. When you have a found the right size drill bit, measure up 1/2 inch from the tip of the end of the bit and mark it with masking tape. In Fig. 24-7 we are drilling in the holes, making sure we don't drill in any further than our mark on the tape.

In Fig. 24-8 we are pounding the nails into place. If you blunt the head of the nail when you are pounding it in, don't try to sharpen it up unless you have pounded it completely flat. This won't happen unless you have a made your holes too small.

If you have any finish sanding to do, complete it at this time. Wax and buff.

Chapter 25

Project 19—
Sea Shell Dish

This project was designed to require you to use the utmost of the carving skills you have learned thus far. This will be true not only in the mechanics of the carving, but in the manner in which you must plan ahead and work on your project as a whole. A set of sea shell dishes would be a beautiful addition to your table used as individual dessert or hors d'oeuvres dishes at a seafood dinner.

Our dish is patterned after the scallop shell. Figure 25-1 is your finished dish. Figure 25-2 is your scale drawing and silhouette view. Note that the scalloped edges of the dish don't show up in either the top or the silhouette view. This is because the scalloped edges will be carved into the front edge of the dish instead of cut in.

When you make your pattern, draw in the circle in the middle of the shell. This is the flat area on the bottom of the dish on which it sits. After cutting out your project on the jigsaw, draw this circle in with pen on the surface you want to be the bottom. Start your carving with a drum sander on the hinge area of the shell as shown in Fig. 25-3. Cut this area down almost as far as you will want it when finished.

CUTTING IN THE GROOVES

Now turn the dish back over and refer to Fig. 25-4. We are going to make eight grooves in the top front edge of the dish to provide the basis of our scalloped edge. You will notice I have penciled in four lines on each side of the center of the dish to give me

Fig. 25-1. Finished sea shell dish.

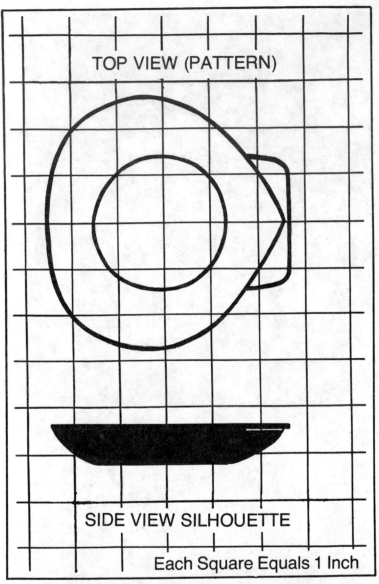

TOP VIEW (PATTERN)

SIDE VIEW SILHOUETTE

Each Square Equals 1 Inch

Fig. 25-2. Scale drawing and silhouette view for sea shell dish.

a help in spacing them out properly. To make your work a little harder, I am not including a pattern for these lines. Study the photographs of the finished dish and Fig. 25-4 and draw in your own lines. Don't cut these grooves in very far at this time, less than one-third the thickness of your piece of wood. Remember, if you cut them in too far, any liquid you have in the dish would run out these grooves. The grooves should be spaced far enough apart to bring a groove up from the bottom and fit in between the grooves on top.

Going on to Fig. 25-5, turn your dish over and start working down the sides of the dish. Remember, the area within the circle you

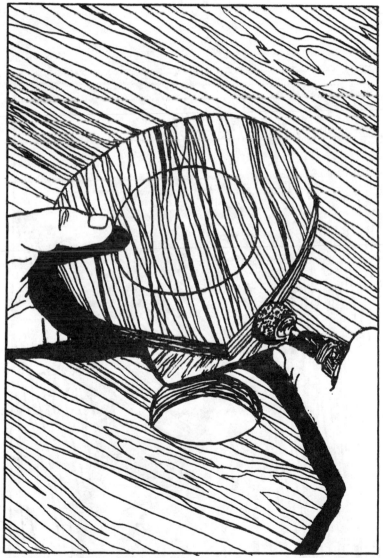

Fig. 25-3. Cut down the hinge area from the bottom. The circle drawn on the bottom will be the flat area for the dish to sit on.

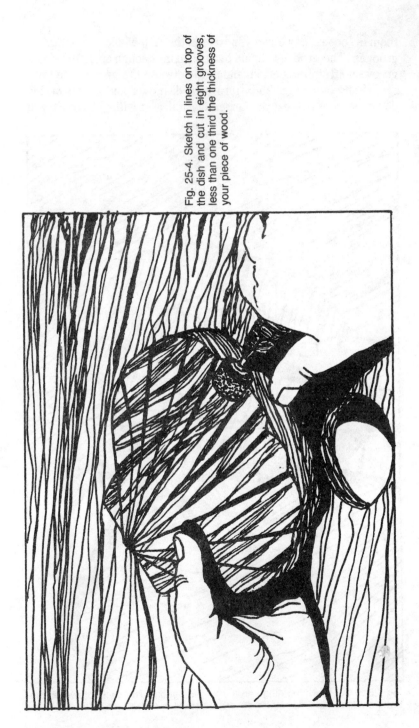

Fig. 25-4. Sketch in lines on top of the dish and cut in eight grooves, less than one third the thickness of your piece of wood.

Fig. 25-5. Work down the bottom sides of the dish up to the circle and almost up to the grooves you have cut in from the top for your scallop effect.

have drawn on the bottom is to remain flat as illustrated. Notice also how you work down the bottom to curve up to the grooves you have cut in from the top. As always leave it thicker than you will want it when finished. Work completely around the dish. Bring your curve up from the flat area to the top edge of the dish and to the hinge area at the back of the dish.

Refer now to Fig. 25-6. We now cut in the grooves from the bottom to fit in between the grooves on top. The grooves will be deepest at the scalloped edge and they get shallower where they disappear into the flat area. Keep working back and forth from the top side to the bottom side to make your scallops even. In Fig. 25-7 we have the scalloped edges pretty well roughed in and have gone back to the sides to make sure they flow into the first scallop in a straight line. Remember, you still have not started hollowing out any of the inside of the dish yet. As with your other projects of this type, you will want to finish up the bottom to an almost finished stage before starting the hollowing-out process.

HOLLOWING OUT THE DISH

Start from the back or hinge area of the dish. In Fig. 25-8 I have worked up about halfway through with my steel oval cutter. Work up fairly close to the edges of your dish. These will be the thinnest of any project you have made so far. In Fig. 25-9 I have worked on over towards the left side and then sanded it down with a #50 grade sandpaper so I can better check the thickness. Now I am starting to work down the rest of the front and the right side of the dish. As you work up to the front, start working from the front back to meet it. As you do this, you will have to work in the grooves to follow the lines of the grooves you have made on the bottom of the dish. This is going to be a little touchier than it was on the bottom. There you were able to use your drum sander. Here you will have to use your steel oval cutter throughout. The grooves, or scallops, must be deepest at the front. Then they get shallower and shallower until they disappear into the bottom of the dish. This will take you a little time and you want to use your cutter as if you were trying to erase a pencil mark from a piece of tissue paper. Don't try to cut down one scallop at a time, but work back and forth across this area.

You might want to stop and go back to the bottom of the dish to deepen one of the grooves just a little. It is a good practice to stop every once in a while and use a piece of sandpaper by hand to take out any bumps you are having trouble with. This allows you to check

Fig. 25-6. Cutting in the grooves on the bottom of the dish to fit in between the grooves you have started on the top.

Fig. 25-7. When grooves have been cut in from the bottom, finish working down the sides to blend into the curve of the grooves.

Fig. 25-8. Hollow out inside of the dish with an oval steel cutter. Work from the back to the front of the dish.

Fig. 25-9. As you hollow out the inside of the dish, work in the grooves on the top so they blend into the bottom of the dish.

on the thickness as you go along. Your dish should be worked down very thin, leaving just enough thickness to keep it from being fragile.

Spend a little extra time with your finish sanding and really work it down to a glassy surface. When finished with your sanding, rub a good coat of Johnson's paste wax into it and buff to a shine.

Again, this project requires you to think ahead just a little all the time. When you cut the grooves in the bottom, you must think about how that is going to affect the grooves you will be cutting in from the top. As you start cutting in the grooves from the top, you must think ahead of how they should shallow out to the bottom of the dish. Work slowly and carefully at all times and you will have a beautiful dish when you are through.

Chapter 26

Project 26— Tiki Salad Service Set

This project is a salad service set with a *Tiki* face carved into the handle. By this time you should be able to look at the photograph of the finished project, the scale drawing of the top and silhouette view and have a pretty good idea of how to proceed. We won't bother to go through any of the steps in carving out the spoon and fork with the exception of two things. First, you will notice that the fork have a lot more curve to them than on your other forks. This is to help in picking up salad from a bowl. Second, when you come to the handle, don't carve down the bottom surface very far. Work down the top side and the end, but leave the bottom about half finished until you have carved in the face. After the face is carved in, then finish the bottom to the desired thickness.

Figure 26-1 is our finished set. Figure 26-2 is our scale drawing and silhouette view of the fork. Figure 26-3 is the scale drawing and silhouette view of the spoon. Our material is 1-inch walnut stock. If you want, and it would be a good idea, get a piece of 1-inch white pine and cut out just a handle to practice on before you actually start carving the face into your walnut spoon and fork. This way you will not ruin your whole project if you have any trouble with the face.

CARVING THE FACE

Study the faces as shown in Fig. 26-1. You will notice that they are slightly different. I did this to provide a little variety in the set. When you draw your pattern from the scale drawing, draw the face

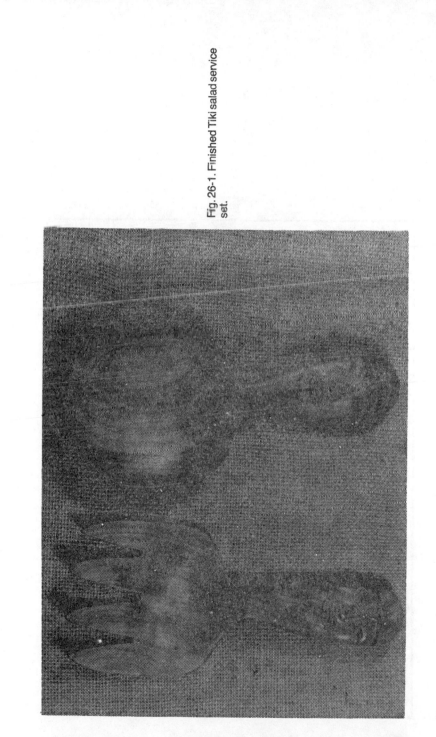

Fig. 26-1. Finished Tiki salad service set.

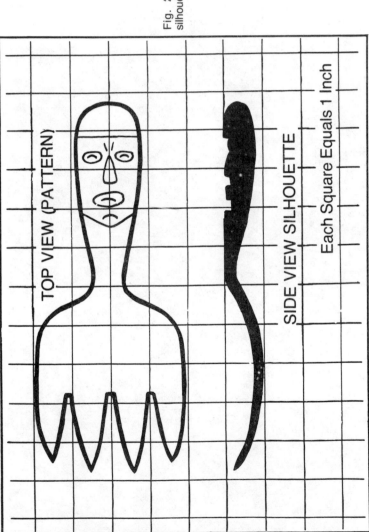

Fig. 26-2. Scale drawing and silhouette of spoon.

TOP VIEW (PATTERN)

SIDE VIEW SILHOUETTE

Each Square Equals 1 Inch

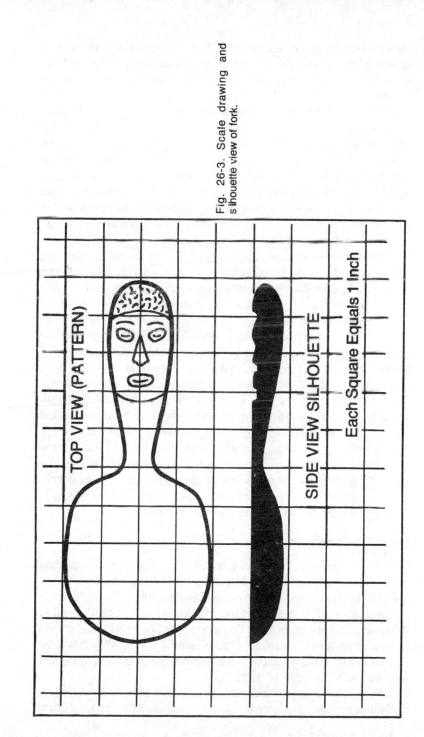

Fig. 26-3. Scale drawing and silhouette view of fork.

TOP VIEW (PATTERN)

SIDE VIEW SILHOUETTE

Each Square Equals 1 Inch

right into the handle of your pattern. The one we will do is the face as shown on the spoon. Don't worry if it does not come out exactly as mine did. The main thing is to get a *Tiki* face recessed into the handle.

Copy your face onto the handle of your spoon or spoon handle. This includes drawing in the line across the forehead, the eye sockets, the slits for the eyes, the nose, the lips, the slit for the mouth and the line across the bottom for the chin. Everything will be recessed from the surface of the handle, except for the nose and lips, which will be on a level with the top, or surface, of the handle. You don't have a lot of depth to work with, so it will actually be a sort of pushed-in face. However, this is the way these faces are carved on the stone statues found in the South Pacific.

Make a cut with the edge of your drum sander across the forehead and the chin. Next, cut out the nose with the edge of your sander. In Fig. 26-4 we have made these cuts and are now recessing a small area for the eye socket on each side of the nose. This is done by laying your drum sander flat on the surface of the face as illustrated. Next, cut around the lips, again with the edge of your drum sander, being careful not to touch the nose as this is done. You won't be able to cut it in perfectly with your drum sander as you don't have enough room. This is only to get the general shape of the face cut in.

Now look at Fig. 26-5 for a moment. The lips have been cut into a rough stage. You will finish up with a pointed X-*acto* knife and sand paper. The area right under the eye socket is left high to denote the cheek bones. It has been sanded down to the depth of the cut you have made around the mouth and then sloped off to the side of the face. The area below the lips will be worked down to the same depth. Use the very edge of your drum sander to make a slight depression on each side of the nose to denote the nostrils.

SMOOTHING DOWN THE FACE

Use a very small steel cutter to cut in the eyes, mouth and eyebrows. Your face is now completely roughed in. Once again, we are back to doing everything by hand sanding. Slope the ends of the forehead area off to the side. Use your knife to finish up the end of the nose and more around the lips if needed. The bridge of the nose should be rounded. You will be surprised how smooth you will be able to get the face by folding over a small piece of sandpaper and working with the edge of it.

When you have the face smoothed down, finish up the bottom of the handle by cutting it down to the desired thickness with your drum

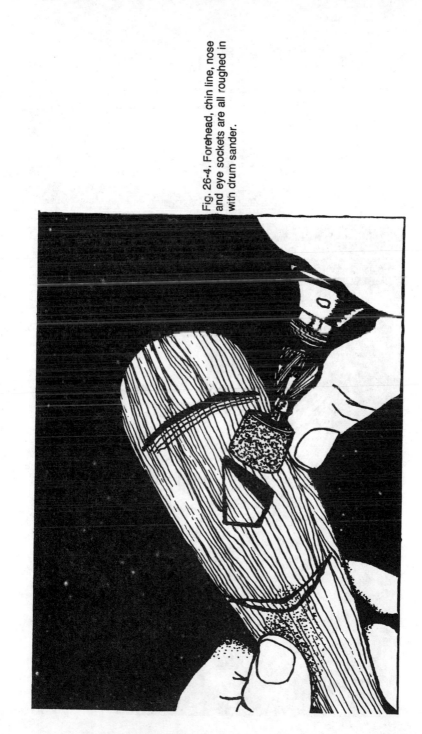

Fig. 26-4. Forehead, chin line, nose and eye sockets are all roughed in with drum sander.

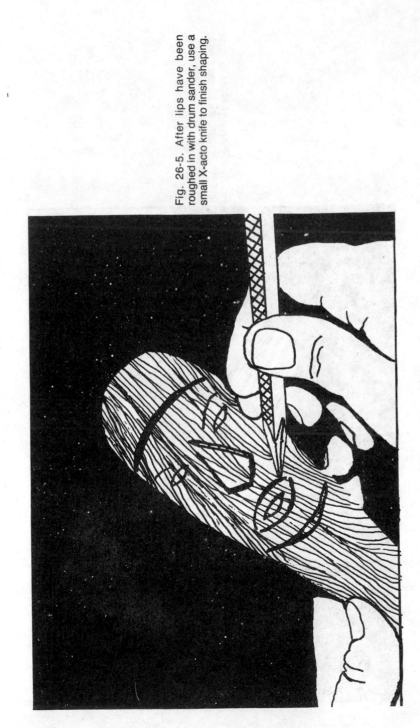

Fig. 26-5. After lips have been roughed in with drum sander, use a small X-acto knife to finish shaping.

sander. The last step is to cut the series of notches in the head to represent the hair. Again, this is done with the edge of your drum sander. Cut these notches in across the front, the sides and the top, but not on the back. Sand, wax, buff and your project is complete.

The face is really quite simple to do, so don't let it throw you. If it doesn't come out exactly as you had it planned, don't worry. Who's going to know except you?

Chapter 27

Project 21—
Wood Jewelry

There are many different kinds and styles of wood jewelry which can be carved with your Moto-tool. If you check your gift shops and magazines, you will find it is very much in fashion these days. These fads of wood, glass and metal jewelry used to go in and out of style with the passing of the seasons. However, nowadays the fashions are "anything goes" and you will find wood jewelry appropriate at any time.

BANGLE BRACELET

First, we will make a bracelet of the bangle type. You can make it as wide or as thin as you desire. Making several bangles of different widths would look very nice when worn with one wide one in the middle and a thin one on each side. Figure 27-1 is our finished bangle. Just to make matters simple, I made this from regular 1-inch walnut stock. Figure 27-2 is your pattern and end view. All you need to do is use a compass to draw a circle on a stiff piece of paper or economy blank cardboard. Cut the center out and try slipping it over the hand of the person you are making it for. The one in Fig. 27-2 might be a little small for most women. I made this for my wife and she has very small hands. A bangle should be just large enough to slip over the hand when the fingers and thumb knuckles are pressed together. When the hand is held in the normal position, the bangle will not slip back over the hand and come off.

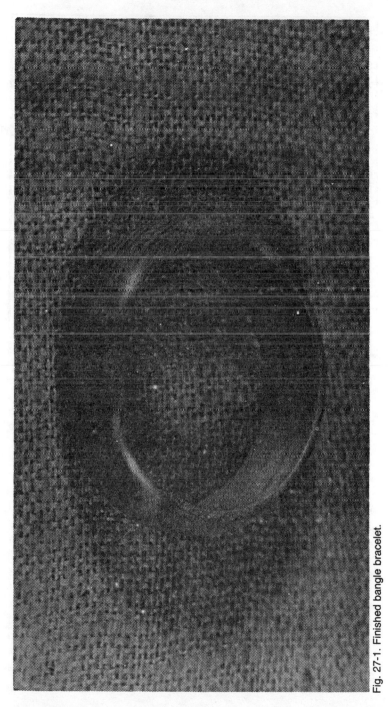

Fig. 27-1. Finished bangle bracelet.

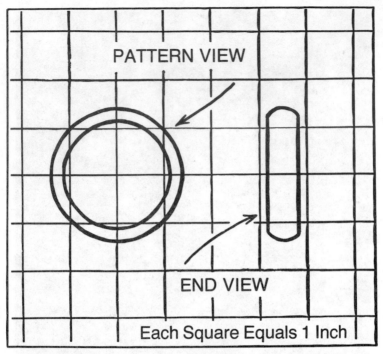

Fig. 27-2. Pattern and end view of bangle bracelet.

Cutting and Sanding

Cut the outside circle of your bangle first. Then drill a hole through the inside so you can slip your jigsaw blade through and cut out the inside circle. Take your time in cutting it out and get it in just as perfect a circle as you can. This will cut down on your sanding time.

When the bangle is cut out, use your sanding drum to work down any outstanding rough spots. Now wrap a piece of #50 or #80 sandpaper around a half-round wood rasp and work down the inside of the bangle until you can slip it over the hand and there are no rough spots left. See Fig. 27-3. Do not round off the edges on the inside.

Now use your sanding block on the outside of the bangle as shown in Fig. 27-4. I would start off with a #80 or a #100 grade of sandpaper unless you have some very rough spots left from cutting it out. Make sure you keep the sandpaper moving around the curve of the bangle at all times so you will not sand in any flat spots. Check to make sure the bangle is the same thickness throughout the complete circle. If it is thicker than you would like it when completed, now is the time to thin it down.

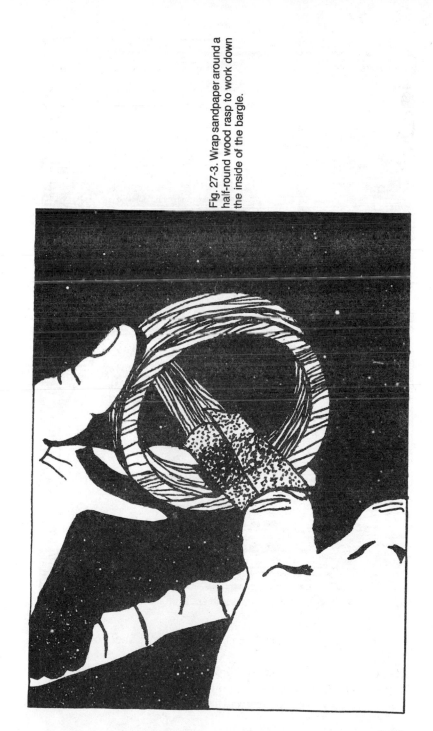

Fig. 27-3. Wrap sandpaper around a half-round wood rasp to work down the inside of the bargle.

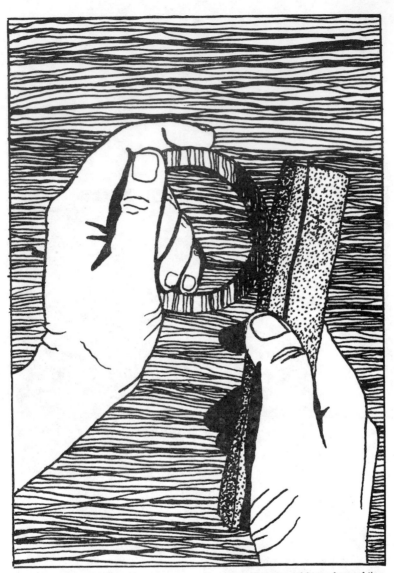

Fig. 27-4. Use sanding block to take rough spots off the outside surface of the bangle.

When this process has been completed, lay a sheet of #100 or #180 grade of sandpaper flat on your workbench and sand down the sides of your bangle as shown in Fig. 27-5. Work down the sides until they are smooth and there are no chipped-out areas which might have occurred when you were cutting out the bangle on your saw.

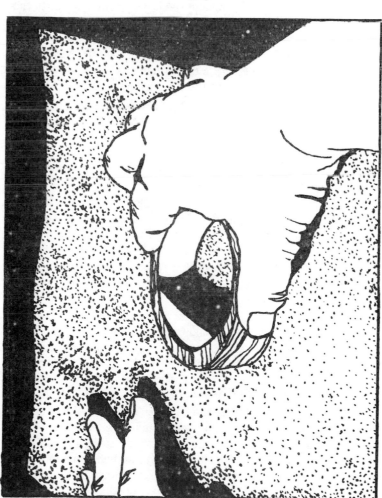

Fig. 27-5. Working down the edges of the bangle.

Laying a piece of sandpaper on your workbench instead of using a sanding block is a sure way of keeping the sides of the bangle perfectly flat as you sand them down. The sides don't have to worked down perfectly smooth at this time. The main purpose is to make them flat and get them ready for the finish sanding.

Curving Off The Top Edge

Now refer to Fig. 27-6. We are using the drum sander to start curving off the top edge of the bangle. You will notice that I have once again drawn a line down the center of the project to give me help in keeping the curve even throughout the circle of the bangle. In the project as illustrated, I have tried to keep the thickness and width of the bangle such that the curve across the top will be an oval shape. This shape seems to present a pleasant appearance. However, this choice is up to you. If your bangle is not quite so thick as shown, you will not have so much curve to the top surface. If the thickness is about as shown, but the width is less, you will have more of a curve to the top surface and it will be almost half-round.

"Raising" the Grain

When you have the edges roughed in with your sanding drum, use your sanding block again to take out any bad rough spots. The finish sanding, from a rough grade of sandpaper to your final smooth grade, will be done without the use of a sanding block. Cup the sandpaper between your fingers and work it down for the finish sanding. This way you will not have any flat spots on the final project. When you have the bangle worked down as smooth as you can get it, rub it down with a wet rag, leaving the wood wet but not "running" wet. Set it aside until thoroughly dry. This will "raise" the grain, which may then be sanded again before waxing and buffing.

Actually, this "raising" should be done to any wood carving if you want the smoothest surface possible. I skip it on most projects which are going to set up on the shelf or not be handled very much. As jewelry is going to be next to, and pick up moisture from, the skin, this process should be followed. It wouldn't hurt to do this several times before you wax and buff the project. If the bangle is worn very much, it will pick up enough moisture from the skin to raise the grain and make it a little rough, even though it has been waxed. Any wood surface which is going to be handled a lot, even though it will be waxed, varnished or painted, should have the grain raised by wetting. Remember, you want to wet it just enough so that

Fig. 27-6. Use your sanding drum to round off the edges on the outside surface of the bangle. Notice reference line drawn around the center of the bangle.

the surface is thoroughly wet, but the wood is not saturated with water throughout. Just as important, let it dry thoroughly before you sand it again.

ITALIAN GOOD LUCK HORN

Another piece of jewelry which can be easily made and which is very much in style for both men and women is an *Italian good luck*

Fig. 27-7. Finished Italian good luck horn.

horn. Figure 27-7 is the finished project and Fig. 27-8 is your pattern. Again, I cut this from regular 1-inch walnut stock. The bellcap on the top was obtained from Grieger's, whose address was included earlier in the book. This can be worn on a silver or bold chain or, if you prefer, you can wear it on a leather thong. I wear mine on a leather thong as it is more in keeping with the "natural" look.

In Fig. 27-9 I have cut out the basic pattern from my walnut stock, drawn my reference line down the center, and then narrowed the point down to the approximate shape shown. From there on, it is just a matter of working it down with a fine, drum sander until you have the shape as shown in Fig. 27-7. I use a fine, drum sander right from the start as there is not too much wood to work with. I want to make sure I don't cut too much from one side by accident. You will want your good luck horn to be as round as possible, still maintaining the curve of the horn.

When you get to the top of the horn, round it off just slightly so that you may bend your bellcap around it without any sharp bends to mar the appearance. When you have the desired shape and have it sanded, wet it down as you did your bangle to raise the grain. Then sand again. This should be done several times, especially on something which is worn around the neck as it will draw more moisture there than any other place.

When this process has been completed, bend your bellcap so that it fits evenly and smoothly with the loop squarely on the top. Glue into place with *epoxy glue*. Let it dry for at least 24 hours before applying the wax. Be sure to buff it down thoroughly. Just to make sure, apply the wax and let it dry, then buff several times. You can't buff it too much as long as you keep it well coated with wax.

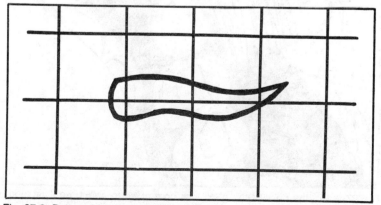

Fig. 27-8. Pattern for Italian good luck horn.

The *Italian good luck horn* which we have illustrated here is about the largest size you would want to make a good appearance. It wouldn't take very much effort to reduce the pattern just a little to produce a smaller one. In fact, you wouldn't have to change the pattern size at all. Just keep working it down until you have a smaller

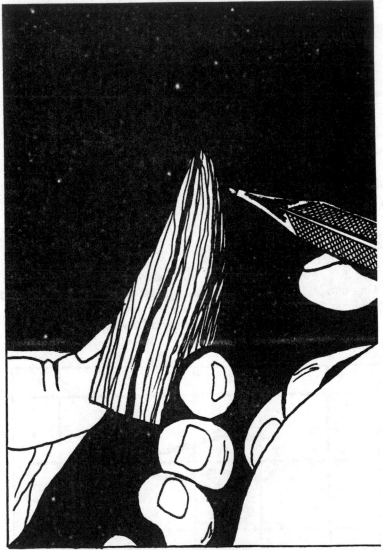

Fig. 27-9. Cut the point of the good luck horn down to about the illustrated thickness before starting the rounding-off process.

size which suits your purpose better. If you want to go a step further, make a smaller pattern and make a pair of drop earrings to match the pendant. You can obtain smaller bellcaps from Grieger's to fit your earrings and fasten them on either clamp-on, screw-on or pierced mountings.

OTHER IDEAS

By now, you should have some ideas of your own as to the many different types of wood jewelry which can be made. You have carved out a seahorse. What is to keep you from making a seahorse pendant and drop earrings? You have carved a *Tiki* face into the handle of your salad service set. This would make a very distinctive pendant and earring set.

The *Tiki* face, seahorse, or any other design of fish, bird or animal will make a very good lapel pin with a pin-back glued on the back. When carving something out for a lapel pin, you will want to carve it out in the same manner as you did your whale plaques. If the pin is flat on the back, it will fit smoothly on your lapel. You can make a beautiful wood bead necklace by alternating colors of wooden beads. You might want to carve a small wooden figure to hang in the center. A brightly colored seashell would look very nice hanging in the center of a wooden bead necklace. Alternating glass beads with your wood beads will provide another variation.

WALNUT RING

Another piece of jewelry which is very nice looking is a ring made of walnut to match your bangles. You will want to make it just as wide as you can without appearing over-sized. All you have to do is to drill a hole through a piece of 1-inch walnut stock. Then work it down with your Moto-tool until it barely fits over your finger when rough carved. Work down the inside of the ring the same way you did your bangle. To make it look very distinctive, set a facet-cut stone in the center of the ring.

As you can see, once you get started making jewelry, one idea leads to another. Before you know it, you will have a whole chest full of jewelry you made yourself.

Chapter 28

Project 22—
Coconut Craft

While not in the usual classification of wood carving, the creation of different objects from the shell of a coconut provides an artistic outlet for those who wish to make something a little different. I suppose a coconut could be called wood, but when you start to work with it you are going to think it is stone. Almost everyone has bought a coconut at the grocery store and wondered how they were going to get it open after they got it home, short of using a sledge hammer.

The shell of a coconut is really amazing when you get right down to it. It apparently will last for years. I have found coconuts floating in the ocean. When opened, the water inside had no salt taste to it whatsoever.

COCONUT GLASS

The coconut is especially adaptable for making dishes, glasses, ash trays and the like. For our first project, let's make a coconut glass. Figure 28-1 shows a coconut glass and an ash tray. Actually, they are made almost the same. Most grocery stores or markets carry coconuts. To make a glass, you will want to pick out a coconut which is more egg-shaped than round. All you have to do is cut off the top, clean out the meat from the inside, and glue the top to the bottom to give it something steady to stand on. You will notice that

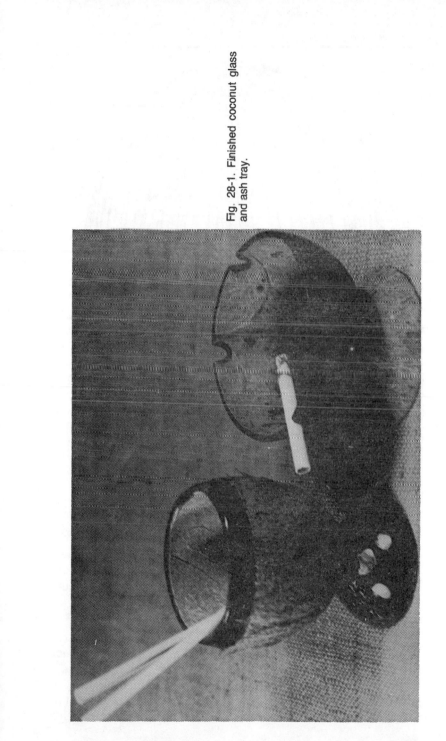

Fig. 28-1. Finished coconut glass and ash tray.

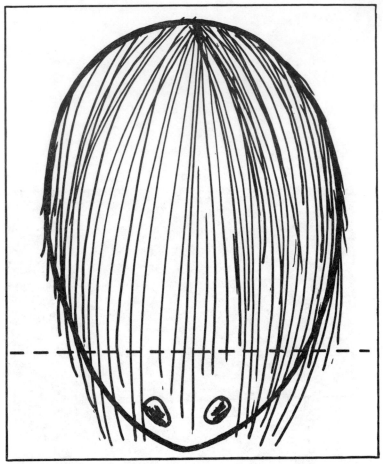

Fig. 28-2. Sketch of coconut and the approximate line it should be cut off on the top to make your glass.

each coconut has three soft spots on the end of the nut. Poke a hole through one of them to allow the water (or milk, as some people call it) to drain out. The portion of the nut which has the three soft spots will be cut off near the end and used as the base of the glass.

Cutting the Coconut

Now look at Fig. 28-2. This is just a rough sketch of the coconut and the approximate line you should cut it to make your glass. Naturally, every coconut is going to be different, so this drawing is just to give you a rough idea. Draw a pencil line around the coconut to indicate where you will want it cut. This may be accomplished with a hack saw, but is much easier and more accurate if you cut it with your Moto-tool, using a circular, steel saw. Be very cautious in doing this. This circular saw will go through your finger a lot faster than it will the coconut. After the coconut has been cut open, clean out all the meat. See Fig. 28-3.

When the inside has been cleaned out, use your drum sander to make a lip around the top of the glass as illustrated in Fig. 28-4. In effect, you are cutting away the husk and getting down to the "wood" of the nut. This is not particularly necessary, but it does add an attractive touch to the glass and also makes a smooth lip from which to drink.

Now take the small part of the nut which was cut and use your drum sander as illustrated in Fig. 28-5 to cut out an area into which the top part of the glass can fit. Go about this slowly and keep setting the top part of the glass into position as you work to see how close a fit you are getting. As the coconut is always a little lopsided, you will find that it will never sit directly in the middle of the bottom part.

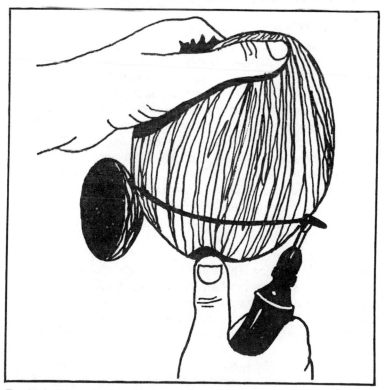

Fig. 28-3. Use a circular saw to cut the coconut.

Fig. 28-4. Cutting in the lip around the top of the glass.

Grinding and Polishing

When this has been accomplished, we are going to grind away all the husk and polish it down as shown in Fig. 28-1. In Fig. 28-6 we are using a disc sander in a hand drill, mounted in a vise. Keep moving the piece of coconut shell around and around so as to prevent too many flat spots. Don't try to sand out all the husk marks as some of them go almost all the way through the shell. The same is true with the two soft spots you have left. You can't sand them all the way out and they only add to the quaintness of the glass.

When you have it worked down to the point where all the loose husk material has been removed, sand it down by hand with a piece of #180 grade of sandpaper to remove any flat spots and also to further smooth it down. The next step is to sand it down to a finished stage with a #600 grade of wet or dry paper, using it wet. You can use a dish pan to work in or just hold it under a faucet with a small stream of water running. This will really put a glassy smooth surface on it and the water doesn't hurt it a bit. You can polish down the whole glass in this manner if you desire. That is up to you. I always think it looks a little more rustic to leave the husk on the top part of the glass. It looks like something you might drink out of if you were in the South Seas.

Now use your disc sander as illustrated in Fig. 28-7 to level off both the top and the bottom parts of the glass. When they have been sanded down perfectly straight, check again to make sure both parts

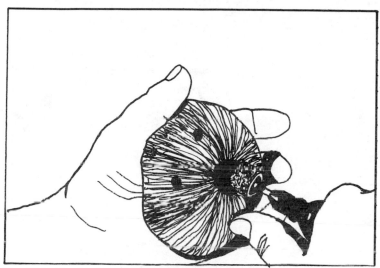

Fig. 28-5. Shaping base for the top of the glass to sit on.

fit together reasonably well and that the glass sits straight. Wet sand the rim around the top of the glass, rounding the edges just slightly.

Gluing the Parts

You are now ready to glue the bottom and top part of the glass together. Again, use *epoxy glue*. Use just a small amount of glue

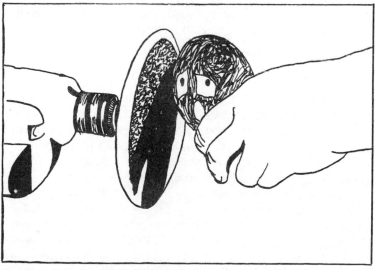

Fig. 28-6. Removing the husk material with a disc sander.

Fig. 28-7. Level the top and bottom surfaces of your coconut glass with a disc sander as illustrated.

around the edge of the hole you have cut in the bottom part. Set the top part of the glass in position and let it dry overnight. Now turn the glass upside down and mix up another batch of glue. Completely cover the area from the bottom, again letting it dry overnight.

When it is dry, spray the polished areas with a clear lacquer to give it a shine. Put on several coats to make sure it is well covered. You need wait only about 20 or 30 minutes between coats when using lacquer.

COCONUT ASH TRAY AND OTHER ITEMS

The ash tray as illustrated in Fig. 28-1 is made in almost the same manner. You will notice I have left the husk material on the base and polished down the ash tray part. The ash tray should be cut from a coconut which has a little rounder shape than the one you used for your glass. The ash tray part should not be as deep. You can cut as many V-notches as you wish around the edges.

Candy and nut dishes may be made in almost the same manner except that the dish part is made by cutting about two-thirds of a coconut shell off lengthwise to provide the dish part. In this case, you will need another coconut to cut off near the end to provide the base, the same as you did for your glass and ash tray. Figure 28-8 shows a candy and nut dish made in this manner. In this case, I have polished

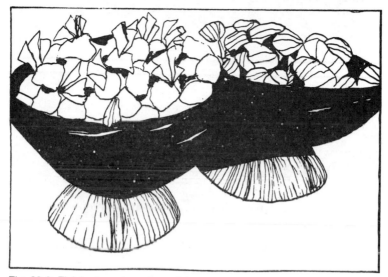

Fig. 28-8. Finished candy and nut dishes.

the dish part down and left the base with the husk material still on it. The nut dish is made from a coconut which was pretty much egg-shaped like you would use for a glass, and the candy dish was made from a coconut which was almost round.

There are a number of items which can be made from the coconut, using the same technique. Make a glass out of a round coconut and it can be used as a planter for either real or artificial plants. Cut the end off a coconut just the same as you would for a glass. Leave off the base, attach three small chains and you have a hanging planter. Find some large, round coconuts and you can make a set of salad dishes. In case you are wondering, you can wash any of the items you make with soap and hot water and they are not harmed in any way.

Chapter 29

Conclusion

You can see there is no end to the things you can carve out which have a practical use as well as being decorative. One of the projects in this book was a small sea shell dish. Using the grid method, enlarge your pattern just a little and use a thicker piece of wood. You will come up with a set of individual salad bowls. Make it larger yet and you will have a salad serving bowl. These, together with your Tiki salad service set, will make a set you can be proud of. Your guests will never guess you made them yourself.

PROJECT SUGGESTIONS

Using the pattern you have made for the small sea shell dish, carve out a dish from a 2-inch piece of material. You will make it in just the same manner except that you will be able to cut the scallops in a little deeper. Now carve out another shell from the same pattern, using a 2-inch piece of material, but without the flat area on the bottom. Fasten the two together with two small brass hinges and you have a sea shell jewelry box. The carving on the top will be different from the one on the bottom in that the scallops will be just the opposite of each other. Where the scallop on the bottom curves up, the one on the top must curve down so they will fit together. The flat, hinge area carved into the back of the shell dish is an excellent place to mount the hinges. The top will also be different in that you can bring the scallops all the way across the top of the shell, where they gradually diminish in size until they melt into the hinge area. If you want, you can glue a small, real shell onto the top, front center of the box to use as a handle to open it. This makes a very unusual jewelry box and any woman would be happy to receive it.

An old fashioned egg cup is another excellent project to try. In making the egg cup, you will hollow out the part for the egg to sit in first, then carve down the outside to match. Hard boil a large egg to use in testing the size of the hollowed-out area as you work. Be sure you use a large egg. If you use a small egg and hollow out the cup to match, sooner or later you will have an egg which will not fit into the cup. If you want, carve a face into the outside of the cup before you work it down. How about an egg cup with feet on the bottom in place of the regular base? This is nothing new as you see cups, coffee mugs and egg cups advertised in a large number of mail order magazines made in the same manner. It's just the idea you have carved it out yourself and maybe embellished on it just a little to suit your own fancy. Another idea for decorating your egg cup is to work in a design like an Easter egg.

A set of measuring cups is another project to try along this same line. Here too, you would hollow out the cup part before working down the outside. Use a metal measuring cup filled with sugar or salt to keep testing the area you are hollowing out for size. As you work, stop every so often and pour in the sugar or salt to see if you are getting close to the proper size. Keep working it down until you can pour in the sugar or salt and have about 1/4 inch left at the top of the cup. After the inside is sized and finish sanded, use a stone cutter to make a small mark around the inside of the rim to indicate the level at which it should be filled to measure 1/4, 1/2 or one cup, etc. There are two different styles of measuring cups you can make. One style is to have all the cups the same depth with a different width across the top opening. The other style and the one I prefer is to have the width of the opening across the top all the same size. Deepen the depth of the cup to make the different sizes. I think they look more attractive hanging on a rack. I also use the same length handle on each one. •

Having carved out a full-figure sea horse letter opener, it should be no trouble for you to make one about 2-1/2 feet tall without the blade part, mount it on a square base trimmed with rope and mount a world globe on the top spine of the head. If you want, change the design just a little to look more like a real sea horse. If you have a large world globe, carve out four sea horses and connect them together by the fins to make a square, four-legged base. In this case, you want to make sure your globe is the type which will rotate up and down as well as around in a circle so that all sections of the globe will be visible.

You have carved a *Tiki* face into the handle of your salad spoon and fork. Now take a piece of 2 × 12 inch material and make a large face exactly like the one you have carved. After the front side of the face is done, hollow out the back side of it a little to make it lighter and you have a *Tiki* or Voodoo mask to hang on your wall.

START WITH SIMPLE PROJECTS

The real secret in getting started in wood carving is to start carving. But start your carving with simple projects. Too many people have come around to me with a picture of an eagle, wings outstretched in flight, or other like object, and wanted me to show them how to carve one out. That is like the piano student we talked about who wanted to learn to play the piano, but wanted to start out by playing Bach instead of learning all the fundamentals first. With the exception of a few gifted people, you just can't start out this way. The approach to wood carving I have presented to you is designed to allow you to carve out something fairly easy, still requiring good technique, yet give you a good product to finish up with. Using the Moto-tool or hobby center to carve with allows you to establish a good feel for what you are doing with your piece of wood. It allows you to work fast enough for you to see the project take shape before your eyes in a short amount of time. All the techniques you have learned from doing the projects presented here can be applied to any other carving you want to do.

At the start of the book, we talked about knowing what your subject looked like before trying to make a carving of it. If you want to carve a horse, study pictures of the horse. Make a pattern of the side view and cut it out, at least in rough form, from your piece of wood. You can carve out almost any object with your Moto-tool, using only the cutters and drum sanders you have used on the projects in this book.

Above all, patience is the key word in learning to do wood carving. Don't be in too much of a hurry. If your project isn't turning out too well, take time to stop and try to figure out what you are doing wrong. If need be, start the project over completely. If you try hard and take your time, you will soon find yourself carving out projects you never thought possible.

MORE CARVING IDEAS

If you are the sportsman type, think of the possibilities open to you with your wood carving talent. That old .22 rifle which always shot so straight can now sport a new stock made to your own liking. It's really not as hard as you might think. Dismantle the rifle, separating the barrel and firing mechanism from the stock. Measure the stock to get the dimensions you will need for a new stock. Make sure the piece of wood you obtain for your stock measures quite a bit more than your old stock so you will have plenty of wood to work with. You might want to carve a pistol grip into the stock. Another way of customizing your stock is to carve in a large cheek plate. Maybe the old stock was really a little too short for your arms and you can lengthen the butt end so it will have the correct length between the butt plate and the trigger for your arm. Another feature you might want to work in is to have the stock run clear out to the end of the barrel so as to give it a little more weight and improve the balance.

When you have decided upon your design and have the type and length stock material you want, use your old stock to obtain the measurements of the inletting you must do. This includes cutting out a groove for the barrel to rest in, cutting in a hole for the firing mechanism and trigger to fit through and a slot for the clip, if your rifle is so equipped. After the inletting has been done, you will want to work down the outside of the stock to the proper thickness around the trigger and clip area first so the trigger guard screws and clip plate will fit properly. Once this has been accomplished, you can proceed to carve down the rest of the stock to fit your personal needs.

If you have a gun cabinet, you can carve out some relief figures of animals or birds to attach to the doors or the sides to dress it up a little. If you really want to get ambitious, carve out the head of a deer, complete with antlers, to attach to the top center of your cabinet. No sportsman's den is complete without a selection of hand carved decoys of different types of ducks. You can go to your local sporting goods store and obtain a cheap decoy to get the general shape of the duck. In carving out your decoys, you will want to make the head and neck in one piece and the body in another piece, then glue them together after they have been rough shaped. Look through hunting and fishing magazines or an encyclopedia to get the colors of the different types of ducks. You can also get the general shape of the different species of ducks from your encyclopedia. Use your stone cutters to undercut the tail and wing feathers in the same manner you undercut the flippers of your whales you made. You can come up with some realistic decoys if you take your time, especially in painting them. I wouldn't advise taking them out and actually using them. Decoys have a way of getting shot up or disappearing in actual use.

Fish

Different kinds of fish can be carved out, painted and mounted on a wall plaque to further decorate your den. If you make them life size, I doubt if anyone could tell them from the real thing. A fish is easy to carve out. The most difficult part will be in researching the type fish you want to mount. Most sporting goods stores have a few mounted fish hanging around on the wall and you can take your pencil and drawing pad with you to sketch the manner in which the fish is curved, the way the mouth is opened on some types and how the fins and tail are stretched out. Again, you can go to your magazines or encyclopedia to get the colors for painting.

If you live in a house with a large stairway, you can decorate it up with your wood carvings. A floral or leaf pattern can be carved into the side of the railing, depending upon the type railing you have. Gargoyles or dragons can be carved out in relief and glued to the corner posts. The head of a Viking, complete with horned helmet, can be attached to the top of the corner post. Maybe you would prefer an owl or a hawk instead of the Viking.

Chess Set

Another good project is to carve out a chess set. There are any number of ways by which you can make a very distinctive chess set. Pick out the theme you would like to follow in your figures and design your chessmen accordingly. You can follow the traditional style or carve out the figures of real kings, queens, knights, etc. You can make the chessmen in the shape of birds or animals if you want. An ambitious project would be to make the figures after the characters in Greek mythology. Put your imagination to work and you can come up with any number of styles.

Now let's go a step further. At the beginning of the book, we talked about using wood which has been thoroughly dried as opposed to "green" wood which will crack as it dries out, unless dried properly. Take a walk out in the woods and you will find plenty of tree branches laying around that are thoroughly dried out. Some of them will be cracked and some not. Most probably they will have a number of small knots on them. Let your imagination run loose and see if you can find one which can be starved into a figure of some kind, taking advantage of all the cracks and knots which are present.

Index

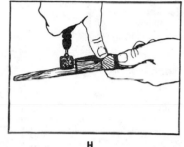